Sergei Eisenstein

Titles in the series Critical Lives present the work of leading cultural figures of the modern period. Each book explores the life of the artist, writer, philosopher or architect in question and relates it to their major works.

In the same series

Jean Genet
Stephen Barber

Jorge Luis Borges
Jason Wilson

Michel Foucault
David Macey

Erik Satie
Mary E. Davis

Pablo Picasso
Mary Ann Caws

Georges Bataille
Stuart Kendall

Franz Kafka
Sander L. Gilman

Ludwig Wittgenstein
Edward Kanterian

Guy Debord
Andy Merrifield

Frank Lloyd Wright
Robert McCarter

Marcel Duchamp
Caroline Cros

Octavio Paz
Nick Caistor

James Joyce
Andrew Gibson

Walter Benjamin
Esther Leslie

Frank Lloyd Wright
Robert McCarter

Charles Baudelaire
Rosemary Lloyd

Jean-Paul Sartre
Andrew Leak

Jean Cocteau
James S. Williams

Noam Chomsky
Wolfgang B. Sperlich

Sergei Eisenstein

Mike O'Mahony

REAKTION BOOKS

Published by Reaktion Books Ltd
33 Great Sutton Street
London EC1V ODX, UK

www.reaktionbooks.co.uk

First published 2008

Printed and bound in Great Britain
by Cromwell Press, Trowbridge, Wiltshire

British Library Cataloguing in Publication Data
O'Mahony, Mike, 1949–
    Sergei Eisenstein. – (Critical lives)
    1. Eisenstein, Sergei, 1898–1948 – Criticism and interpretation
    2. Eisenstein, Sergei, 1898–1948
    3. Motion picture producers and directors – Soviet Union – Biography
    I.Title
    791.4'3'0233'092

ISBN-13: 978 1 86189 367 3

Contents

Sergei Eisenstein during the Making of *October*.

Prologue

And just think!

None, none of this might ever have happened!

None of the sufferings, searchings, heartaches, or spasmodic moments of creative joy! And all because there was an orchestra playing at the Ogins' dacha at Majorenhof.[1]

Thus Eisenstein begins a short passage, titled 'Pre-Natal Experience', in his memoirs. Here, in a few brief sentences, the author has fully whetted the appetite of the reader, introducing an enticing, mysterious narrative of intrigue that would grace the pages of any 'penny dreadful' typical of the fin-de-siècle world into which Eisenstein was born. In the same dramatic vein he continues:

Everyone had drunk far too much that evening. A fight broke out and someone was killed.

Papa grabbed his revolver and dashed across Morskaya Street to restore order.

Mama, who was pregnant with me, was scared to death and almost gave birth prematurely.

A few days passed in the fear of possible *fausses couches* [miscarriage].

But that did not happen.

I made my entrance into this world at the allotted hour, albeit three whole weeks early.[2]

When Sergei Mikhailovich Eisenstein was born on 23 January (10 January old style) 1898, it may, or may not, have been in the wake of such dramatic events as these. Did his father, a civil engineer by trade, really carry a revolver at all times, and was he really so willing to dive into such a dangerous situation without consideration for his own safety? And if such an incident did occur, did it truly instigate such a dramatic, cliff-hanging moment, the future film director's very existence swinging precariously in the balance, his mother on the brink of losing her only son before his birth? We can, of course, never know the answers to these questions. However, the main concern is less whether or not such events actually took place than how Eisenstein's reconstruction of his personal history has shaped our understanding of his life and work. Eisenstein's memoirs, written between 1 May and 12 December 1946 while he was recuperating from a heart attack suffered earlier that year, were never published in his lifetime. However, in the years since his death, various parts of his unfinished manuscript have entered the public domain (here all Eisenstein scholars must offer huge thanks to the Herculean efforts of Naum Kleiman and Richard Taylor for bringing this material to light).

While Eisenstein's memoirs offer fascinating insights into the life and practice of the Soviet filmmaker, it should be noted that his text is notoriously full of anecdotes and contradictory interpretations. As his biographer Oksana Bulgakowa has suggested, Eisenstein's memoirs adopt the form of a *Bildungsroman*, with various episodes presented as trials which the hero overcomes on his journey to character formation and maturity.[3] Further, Eisenstein regularly employs conventional psychoanalytical tropes sometimes to allude to, at other times more explicitly to explain, his personality traits and the many crises in his life. He is variously brutalized by his father, abandoned by his mother, embraced and then rejected by his peers. His relationships with both men and women, as far as can be discerned, are strained and seemingly largely unfulfilled, and, towards the end of his life, even his relationship with the Soviet leader Iosif Stalin takes on the characteristics of a typical parent–child (Oedipal) conflict. Other seemingly profound childhood experiences are introduced as vital to his later development. For example, as a scientific materialist and self-confessed atheist, Eisenstein was a harsh critic of religion and spirituality, and yet religious rituals and biblical references permeate his works to such an extent that he was frequently criticized for excessive religious zeal by the Soviet censors. In this context, he recalls his nanny, who prayed daily before an icon of the Virgin Mary, and Father Pavel of the Suvorov Church in St Petersburg, who 'went through Holy Week as if suffering the Lord's Passion', and whose 'forehead exuded droplets of blood in the candlelight when he read the Acts of the Apostles'.[4] From this perspective, Bulgakowa's allusion to Eisenstein's life history as 'the novel of a narcissist' is both evocative and accurate, and reminds us that both his memoirs and later biographies should be read with a degree of caution.[5]

Yet it might also be added that Eisenstein's memoirs – though sometimes factually unreliable – nonetheless cast intriguing light on other important aspects of his life and work. For example, in the anecdote outlined above he deploys a dramatic story as an illustration of a wider set of problems and dilemmas. Throughout his adult life, Eisenstein struggled to resolve many contradictions, not least his own official support for the Soviet regime and its advocacy of materialism and collectivism, alongside his fascination for Freudian psychoanalysis with its emphasis on the individual psyche. Thus Eisenstein continues by trying to explain away the significance of the prenatal trauma he recounts: 'It is of course hard to imagine that this episode could have left any impression on me *avant la lettre*.'[6] Yet, in contradiction of this statement, he is also quick to point out: 'my haste, and my love of gunshots and orchestras have remained with me ever since. Not one of my films goes by without a murder.'[7] Indeed, cruelty and violence permeate all of Eisenstein's films, from the massacre of the workers in his first production, *Strike*, to the murder of Vladimir Staritsky in his last film, *Ivan the Terrible*. Perhaps the real questions about him are: Is this fascination with brutality the lasting legacy of such a dramatic prenatal experience? Or might it alternatively be a reflection of the politically turbulent, all too frequently violent, times through which he lived?

In what follows, I shall be offering an account of Eisenstein's life coupled with an analysis of his major works. With regard to the first task, I shall not be seeking, as many have before me, to psychoanalyse my subject. The extent to which Eisenstein's emotional experiences may or may not have directly shaped his work is as much a mystery to me as it is, I would argue, to others, despite claims to the contrary. Nor, it might be added, shall I be giving extensive attention to the question of Eisenstein's sexuality, a subject that has obsessed many an author before this one. While the limited evidence available suggests that he probably had sexual relationships with both men and women, these, it seems, were sporadic and rare events in his life. I do not dismiss Eisenstein's sexuality as irrelevant; such a claim would be patently absurd. Sexual identity, along with political, ideological and class identity, are clearly important factors in shaping individuals and thus their engagement with the world as articulated through their art. Rather, I simply acknowledge that insufficient evidence remains to offer a definitive statement on the matter.

I shall therefore be giving greater priority, as far as is possible, to the material facts of Eisenstein's life, the wider socio-historical context in which he lived and operated, and, most importantly, to the works themselves, the product of that existence. Following the conventions of much biographical writing, I shall adopt a broadly chronological approach examining, in turn, Eisenstein's childhood and youth, early professional experiences as a young adult and his mature career up to his untimely death in 1948, barely a month after his fiftieth birthday. To highlight the necessarily contingent nature of this task, however, and to embrace Eisenstein's own sense, and literary reconstruction, of his life as a series of dramatic performances, I shall structure what follows into five chapters or acts, each examining a key period in his life and focusing on major works produced during that period.

Eisenstein's output was both extensive and diverse. He was a prolific writer, an avid artist – producing hundreds of drawings at different stages of his career – and, of course, a major filmmaker. While these works undeniably bear the hallmarks of a highly individual and experimental mind, I shall also argue that, despite their seemingly universal appeal, they were very much the product of the time and place in which they were made, namely the Soviet Union under Stalin. This, I would contend, left an indelible mark upon Eisenstein's entire creative output.

1

Experimentation

By any measure, the young Sergei Eisenstein's childhood would have to be described as one of social and economic privilege. He was born in 1898 in the Latvian city of Riga, then a thriving if somewhat provincial outpost in the Russian Empire, the only child of parents who had forged what was widely held at the time to be the perfect combination of status and wealth. Mikhail Osipovich Eisenstein came from a German-Jewish family that had recently converted to Christianity and had rapidly climbed the social ladder. Both of his brothers, Dmitry and Nikolai, had risen to positions of authority, the former an officer in the Tsarist army, killed in the Russo–Japanese War in 1904, the latter a judge. In 1893, Eisenstein senior graduated from the St Petersburg Institute of Civil Engineering and was, shortly thereafter, sent to Riga. There, over the next quarter-century, he rose to become the city's chief engineer and then official architect, on the way attracting decorations and a noble rank that entitled him to be addressed as 'Your Excellency'. In 1897 he married the younger Yulia Ivanovna Konetskaya, the daughter of a wealthy St Petersburg merchant. Where Sergei Eisenstein's father brought social status and reputation to the family, his mother contributed economic prosperity and the passion for all things European that so typified the Russian fin-de-siècle haute bourgeoisie.

In this cosy environment, the young Sergei was raised in the style typical of the very class that so many of his early movies

Sergei Eisenstein with his father Mikhail Osipovich Eisenstein, Riga, 1904.

sought to demonize. He was educated at home by private governesses in a household that also boasted a servant, a cook and a housemaid. In addition, he was personally tended to by his Latvian nanny, Maria Elksene. His early education, too, was largely typical of the Russian bourgeoisie. His days were spent learning to dance, skate, ride horses and play the piano. He took up drawing from an early age and, according to his childhood friend and later acting colleague Maxim Straukh, spent much of his time filling exercise books with sketches. Eisenstein also read a lot, familiarizing himself with European culture. By the age of eleven he was already able to speak Russian, German, French and English, using his linguistic skills to access such writers as Dostoevsky, Zola and Dickens in the original. Later, when studying at the *Realschule* in Riga, he developed broader interests in mathematics and science.

In 1906 the Eisensteins travelled to Paris, a typical enough journey for a family of their social standing. The French capital had long been a magnet for wealthy Russian society, attracting regular tourists and establishing a thriving community of expatriates, including artists and writers, many of whom gathered around the numerous Russian libraries, cafés and clubs.[1] The presence of so many Russians in Paris at this time reflected the close ties between the two nations, formalized eight years earlier with the signing of the Franco–Russian Alliance. Indeed, the Pont Alexandre III, opened in time for the 1900 International Exposition, notably symbolized the entente between the two nations. Recognized for both its engineering achievements and its extravagant Art Nouveau decoration, this structure must have appealed greatly to Eisenstein's father, whose affection for Art Nouveau was later cruelly condemned by his son.[2] Russian cultural achievements were also very much in vogue in Paris at the time of the Eisensteins' visit. That summer the impresario Sergei Diaghilev staged a major exhibition of Russian art at the Petit Palais, the catalyst for his return in 1909 to launch the first season of the famous *Ballets Russes*.

The obvious attractions of Parisian culture may, in themselves, have been sufficient to attract the Eisensteins. However, the political destabilization and social unrest back home following Russia's defeat in the Russo–Japanese War and the Revolution of 1905 may also have provided motivation to spend time abroad. Even in provincial Riga, strikes and bloody conflicts between the authorities and Revolutionary supporters were not infrequent between 1905 and 1907.[3] Whatever the reasons for the trip, it certainly shielded the young Sergei from many of the horrors of Revolutionary politics as well as providing him with a host of new experiences. These included visits to Napoleon's tomb and the

Musée Grevin, where, as he later recounted, he was fascinated by the waxwork models, especially those displaying scenes of torture and execution. It was also during this Parisian sojourn that Eisenstein saw his first film, attending a screening of Georges Méliès's *400 farces du diable* at a cinema on the Boulevard des Italiens.

Beneath the surface of Eisenstein's idyllic childhood, however, domestic tensions were much in evidence as the ties that bound his parents were revealed to be decidedly fragile. Rows were an all too common occurrence in the Eisenstein household, and in 1909 the couple were divorced. The reasons for this are usually ascribed to Yulia Ivanovna's unfaithfulness; she is reputed to have had an affair with her husband's cousin. Perhaps inevitably, biographical studies have made much of this circumstance and its potential impact on the formation of the young Eisenstein's character. There can, of course, be little doubt that such domestic circumstances must indeed have been traumatic for the boy, who was later to attribute his 'corrupted . . . belief in the foundations of the family' to his parents' divorce.[4] However, one should not entirely overlook the fact that his abandonment was perhaps not as extreme as some writers have made out. Like many children of the Russian bourgeoisie, Eisenstein was raised and nurtured more extensively by his nanny than by his mother and doubtless turned to the former for emotional support and sustenance. Furthermore, he remained in regular contact with his mother after her separation from his father, visiting her often in St Petersburg and holidaying with her. When in 1915 he moved to Petrograd (as St Petersburg was renamed at the start of the First World War), he went to live with his mother, retaining a close bond with her throughout the rest of her life. Similarly, a great emphasis has been placed upon the overbearing nature of his father – Eisenstein later claimed that 'a tyrannical Papa was commonplace in the nineteenth century, but mine dragged on into the twentieth.'[5] Once again it might be worth giving consideration to the fact that Eisenstein's condemnation, both public and private, may have had much to do with distancing himself from his father's overt support for the Tsarist regime, both before and after the Bolshevik Revolution. After all, at this time, the class origins of the father were held by many to leave an indelible mark on the son. None of this is to diminish the importance of the breakdown of his parents' marriage, but rather to indicate that these traumatic childhood experiences were far from the only factors that contributed to the ultimate development of Eisenstein's character. Indeed, far greater consideration needs to be given to the socio-political and cultural milieu in which he was raised.

If the young Eisenstein's privileged upbringing largely shielded him from the instability and unrest that characterized Russian society in the years preceding the First World War, it brought him into direct contact with the cultural developments of the so-called 'Silver Age'. While the social structures that held Tsarist society together were unravelling, Russian culture was entering a period of rapid transformation, even a flowering. In literature, poetry and music this was a time of experimentation and innovation, as attested to by the works of such luminaries as the writers Andrei Bely, Dmitry Merezhovsky and Alexander Blok, and the composers Pyotr Tchaikovsky, Nikolai Rimsky-Korsakov and Igor Stravinsky. In the visual arts too, the social realism of the *peredvizhniki*, or Wanderers, that had dominated mid- to late nineteenth-century painting, was giving way to the more esoteric, individually inspired Symbolism characterized by the works of Alexander Benua, Viktor Borisov-Musatov and the *Mir Iskusstvo* group, or to the Russian folkloric tradition of the Abramtsevo artists' colony. A fascination with a mythical, fairy-tale vision of ancient Rus was also evident in architecture as native styles coalesced with influences from Art Nouveau to create a new architectural vocabulary epitomized by the exotic fantasies of Fyodor Shekhtel.

Nowhere was this transformation felt more acutely than in the theatre. As Konstantin Rudnitsky has pointed out, the period between 1905 and 1917 was one in which the theatre

> was the subject of endless discussion and furious debate by people who had momentarily forgotten their usual pursuits, who had either no links at all with the theatre or who had come into contact with the stage only accidentally, peripherally . . . It was as if Russia's historical fate depended on solving the problem of the theatre.[6]

This was the era of Chekhov and Stanislavsky at the Moscow Arts Theatre; of Meyerkhold's early experiments in the psychology of movement; and of Tairov's experimental productions at the Kamerny Theatre. The period immediately prior to the First World War was also the era of the Futurists Vladimir Mayakovsky, Alexei Kruchenykh and Velimir Khlebnikov, whose performances, including *Vladimir Mayakovsy – A Tragedy* and *Victory Over the Sun*, both courted and gained notoriety. Against a backdrop of ever more stringent state censorship, what united the disparate approaches of these writers and directors was a belief in the transformative capabilities of the theatre and a desire to bring theatrical performances to new audiences, indeed to the masses. The philosopher Vyacheslav Ivanov even proffered the idealistic vision that collective theatrical performance could act as a catalyst for the revolutionary transformation of humankind.[7] All of this formed the cultural backdrop to Eisenstein's personal development.

From his early youth Eisenstein regularly attended performances at the main theatres in both Riga and St Petersburg, experiences that clearly made a major impression on him. As Straukh has pointed out, he and Eisenstein often discussed, even re-enacted, performances they had seen, while Eisenstein's early interests in staging and costume design were expressed in numerous drawings and even the games he played with toy soldiers. Theatre, however, was not the only form of entertainment to attract popular audiences in late Tsarist Russia. The circus also drew large crowds, not least among the growing urban workforce. Yet the circus was far from an entertainment devised for, or attended exclusively by, this social group. Whether admired for the sheer skill of its performers or for the exotic, often erotic, charms of the performers, circuses attracted audiences from widely divergent classes. The young Eisenstein frequently attended circus performances, sometimes with his nanny, other times with his father, who reputedly loved the equestrian skills of dressage riders.[8] Eisenstein's passion for the circus, as we shall see, was to play a major part in his early work in both the theatre and the cinema.

Nor was the circus the only form of popular entertainment to entice audiences from across the social spectrum. In May 1896, the first film screening took place in Russia, presented as a novelty at a summer amusement park in St Petersburg.[9] Within two decades, the Empire boasted over 4,000 movie theatres with 229 in Petrograd alone.[10] Although dominated in the early days by foreign imports, the first native film studio was established in 1907, also in St Petersburg, and it was then that the history of filmmaking in Russia began in earnest. The rapid expansion of cinema as a form of popular entertainment was not initially welcomed universally. For example, the last Tsar, Nikolai II, decried cinema as 'an empty, totally useless and even harmful form of entertainment'.[11] Others expressed fears that viewing moving images could damage the eyes. The greatest concern, however, was cinema's potential to corrupt, both morally and politically. In an era when any gathering of workers was feared, the possibility of the cinematic medium being used, or abused, to disseminate revolutionary ideas to the masses was foremost in the minds of many critics. That the first Soviet leader, Vladimir Ilych Lenin, would later cherish cinema precisely for its potential propaganda values, and that Eisenstein's own films would be seen as fulfilling this vital role, perhaps suggests that the Tsarist ruling classes were not so far off the mark.

Despite such 'dangers', the bourgeoisie flocked to the cinema in their thousands, though preferring to frequent the more exclusive theatres designed (and priced, one must assume) to discourage mixing of the classes. In this respect, the young Eisenstein appears once more to have been largely typical of his class. Though clearly regarding theatre as more vital than cinema at this early point in his life, he was a regular cinemagoer, his memoirs recounting the wide range of films he saw during his youth.

On 2 June 1914, Eisenstein completed his studies at the *Realschule* in Riga. By this time, political tensions in Europe were sufficient to cause the cancellation of a proposed European tour that his mother had planned for the two of them. Despite the outbreak of war less than two months later, the sixteen-year-old Eisenstein seems once more to have been largely unaffected by political turmoil as he completed a year's preparatory study before following in his father's footsteps and enrolling at the Petrograd Institute of Civil Engineering. Here, between 1915 and the beginning of 1917, he divided his time between his technical studies and his passion for the theatre, attending numerous productions by the two foremost directors and drama theoreticians of the period, Vsevolod Meyerkhold and Nikolai Yevreinov, both of whom were greatly to influence his early career.[12]

By his own admission, Eisenstein's schooldays had been unremarkable; the 'horribly exemplary little boy', as he later described himself, had largely followed the path laid out for him by his parents.[13] His cultural interests were not, as yet, part of his professional ambitions. And while his youth had coincided with a time of radical social and cultural transformation, his move from adolescence to adulthood took place against an even more fraught historical moment.

To claim that the Revolutionary events of 1917 were greatly to influence his life is perhaps to state the obvious. Given the magnitude of the social and political transformation brought about by the Tsar's abdication, followed by political unrest, mass strikes, bloody street battles, abortive insurrections from both the left and the right and, finally, the overthrow of the short-lived Provisional Government by revolutionaries promising peace, bread and land to the workers and peasants, it is difficult to imagine how anyone, least of all someone raised as a member of the class overthrown by the Revolution, could remain unaffected. Yet, initially at least, this seems very much to have been the case. Indeed, Eisenstein's lack of interest in the February Revolution might best be gauged by Straukh's account of his friend walking through the fighting on the streets of Petrograd on the eve of the insurrection simply to get to the Imperial Alexandrinsky Theatre to see a production of Lermontov's *Masquerade.* This event, in which Meyerkhold himself played the part of a Blue Pierrot, thus introducing a character from the Italian commedia dell'arte onto the Russian stage, was seemingly of much greater interest to Eisenstein than the fall of the Romanov dynasty. Nonetheless, the radical changes brought about as a consequence of the February Revolution would, in due course, expose him to new experiences and new opportunities.

One immediate consequence of the collapse of the old regime was its impact upon Eisenstein's education. Shortly after the fall of the Tsar, students at the Institute of Civil Engineering were recruited into a local militia and drafted into the army. However, Eisenstein's military experiences at this time kept him far from the dangers of Russia's Western Front. While attending the Ensigns' Engineering School, he was left with plenty of free time. Inspired by the plethora of political cartoons that filled the pages of the Revolutionary press in the wake of relaxed censorship laws, he turned his hand to producing caricatures. He even managed to sell one drawing of the Provisional Government leader Alexander Kerensky to the *Peterburgskaya Gazeta.* Submitted under the pseudonym 'Sir Gay' though not published, this work might be considered his first, albeit tentative, venture into a career in the arts and explicit political commentary.[14]

Eisenstein remained in Petrograd between the February and October Revolutions of 1917. During the summer he was present at the demonstrations and street battles, subsequently dubbed the July Days, and later reported that he had to dive for cover when the firing started.[15] Yet he appears to have witnessed relatively few of the events that led up to the storming of the Winter Palace on 7 November 1917 (25 October old style). Consistent with his habit of missing such moments, he spent that evening at his mother's house sorting through a collection of eighteenth-century engravings. Despite this, his presence in what was then the Russian capital throughout these momentous days certainly helped him, a decade later, to gain the commission to make *October*, the famous cinematic dramatization of this stormy period in Russia's history. While Eisenstein had shown relatively little interest in politics in general, or Bolshevism in particular, up to this time, things were set to change.

When Lenin's Bolshevik Party seized power in October 1917, the future for the young Eisenstein looked decidedly bleak. The initial euphoria that had accompanied the victory of the Revolution was rapidly followed by the collapse of an already frail economic infrastructure, resulting in major food shortages and bringing severe deprivation to both city and countryside. Facing oppositional forces from both inside the former Russian Empire and beyond its borders, the new state embarked upon a brutal and bloody civil war that was to claim the lives of millions as a result of terror campaigns, famine and the rampant spread of disease. The Civil War divided the nation and generated rifts within communities. As Eisenstein was personally to discover, it also tore families asunder. In February 1918, when German forces occupied Riga, his father found himself not only geographically but also politically separated from his son. Remaining true to his capitalist principles, Mikhail

Sergei Eisenstein (right) with fellow soldiers, *c.* 1919.

Osipovich opposed the Revolution and joined the White Army as an engineer. When the Bolsheviks regained control of Riga later that year, he effectively became an enemy of the state and was forced to abandon his homeland or face arrest. He moved to Germany with his new companion Elizaveta Michelson, dying there less than two years later.

The military experiences of the younger Eisenstein were in marked contrast. Within a few months of the Revolution, he was once more drafted into military service, between March 1918 and September 1920 travelling around Russia as an engineer serving in Trotsky's newly formed Red Army. Once more his postings kept him away from combat situations. Protected from the worst excesses of poverty by the money his mother continued to send him, Eisenstein was nonetheless exposed for the first time to some of the world's harsher realities. As an experienced, if not fully qualified, engineer, he was sent variously to Gatchina, Pskov, Izhora, Voshega, Velikie Luki, Kholm and Dvinsk, where he participated in the construction of bridges and defensive fortifications. Despite this service to the state, and his later claims that the Revolution galvanized his political opinions, there is little evidence that Eisenstein rushed to become a fully committed supporter of the new regime. He rarely attended political meetings and spent far more time reading the works of Meyerkhold and Yevreinov than Marx and Engels. As Oksana Bulgakowa has noted, he even dabbled in occultism at a time when such esoteric activities were heavily frowned upon.[16] However, where Eisenstein's direct engagement in Revolutionary politics was conspicuous by its absence, his embracing of Revolutionary culture was to be of great significance. He was soon taking full advantage of the cultural opportunities afforded him by the new regime.

Long before the cruiser *Aurora* fired its fateful shot across the bows of the Winter Palace, thus sparking, symbolically at least, the Bolshevik uprising, Russian revolutionaries had been giving serious consideration to the importance of cultural activity to society as a whole. The main question, here, was what form such cultural activity might take in the wake of the transformed social, political and economic conditions brought about by revolution. On one side of the divide lay those who believed that the main mission lay in bringing traditional culture to the masses. Economic exploitation and class division, they argued, had deprived the working and peasant classes of access to education and thus the potential to appreciate the fruits of civilized culture. Therefore the objective, perceived as a corrective, was to introduce the classics of literature, theatre, art and music to the masses. In essence, the ideal here was the factory worker who could quote Shakespeare or Pushkin, whistle a melody from Beethoven or Tchaikovsky, and admire a painting by Rembrandt or Repin. Yet, such a strategy was rejected by other revolutionary thinkers who condemned such aspirations as a patronizing attempt to 'elevate' the masses, and inculcate in them middle-class customs and values. Instead they advocated the formation of a new, essentially proletarian, culture produced by the masses, for the masses. In this context, the culture inherited from the pre-Revolutionary past was at best suspect, a symptom and product of bourgeois society, and therefore essentially reflective of bourgeois ideology.

On the more traditional side of the debate sat Lenin, long an admirer of Russia's cultural heritage and opponent of the more extreme avant-garde. Indeed, Lenin's personal experiences when he was exiled in Zurich – at the same time that the Dadaists were performing their absurdist theatre, reading noise poems and deliberately abusing audiences at the infamous Cabaret Voltaire – may well have reinforced his resistance to such experimental activities. Once in power, the Bolsheviks established an official administrative body, Narkompros (People's Commissariat of Enlightenment), headed by the one-time Symbolist playwright Anatoly Lunacharsky, to oversee the organization of theatres, orchestras, museums, book publishing and all other related cultural activities. Lunacharsky, like Lenin, recognized the value of the cultural legacy inherited from the old regime. However, his aim was not simply to present it to the previously excluded masses; he sought to re-evaluate this legacy and redeploy it specifically to serve the newly enfranchised working class. Thus, any pre-Revolutionary cultural activity that could be reinterpreted as reflecting a Revolutionary ideology was welcomed into the fold. This more liberal attitude towards cultural heritage was opposed by the more radical theories of Alexander Bogdanov, the founder of the organization known as Proletkult, an acronym derived from the phrase 'proletarian cultural-educational organizations'. Formed just days before the October Revolution,

Proletkult soon became a huge institution, boasting 400,000 members in 300 branches spread throughout the newly formed Soviet lands.[17] For Bogdanov, cultural transformation was as integral an aspect of the Revolution as political and economic transformation, and needed to be just as radical. In essence, Proletkult sought to develop a new, explicitly proletarian culture. Thus it encouraged workers to write novels about factory life, or to form amateur theatrical groups and produce plays highlighting revolutionary experiences. For Proletkult, this new culture was to be much more than a reflection of the values and aspirations of the new ruling class. It was to provide the means of trans-forming the new society, an ideal strikingly echoing Ivanov's pre-Revolutionary conception of the future potential of theatre.

As Lynn Mally has shown, the sheer scale and distribution of Proletkult during the early Bolshevik period ensured that its practices were frequently more diverse, and less ideologically consistent, than might be assumed. Thus, where some branches rejected all past culture and excluded any individual who could not prove his or her proletarian origins, others embraced the classics of the Tsarist era and welcomed members regardless of their previous class identity.[18] This flexibility was vital for the young Eisenstein, who, under the auspices of Proletkult, was given his first significant break in theatre. Furthermore, Proletkult's support for cinema as a potentially democratic medium facilitated their financial support for his first film, *Strike* (1925).

Eisenstein's first practical encounter with Revolutionary culture occurred in January 1920, when he joined the amateur theatrical troupe organized by the Corps of Engineers in Velikie Luki. Here he participated variously as actor, director and stage designer in several productions including Arkady Averchenko's *The Double* and Nikolai Gogol's *The Gamblers*.[19] There is insufficient evidence to offer much insight into Eisenstein's contribution to these early productions. However, his stage designs soon caught the eye of the artist Konstantin Yeliseyev, at that time acting as theatre director at the local House of Culture. As a former pupil of Nikolai Rerikh, notorious for his stage and costume designs for Igor Stravinsky's revolutionary *Ballets Russes* production of *The Rite of Spring*, Yeliseyev's background was unlikely to endear him to the new regime. Nonetheless, he was quick to throw his hat into the Bolshevik ring.[20] In the spring of 1920, he was serving as director to theatrical units attached to the Red Army and invited Eisenstein to join him as a stage and costume designer. He even secured Eisenstein's release from the Corps of Engineers, despite the reticence of his unit commander, who valued the young man far more as an engineer than as an artist.

Eisenstein's decision, following this appointment, to abandon engineering for a career in the theatre has been seen by many of his biographers as a natural progression of his childhood fascination with theatrical spectacle or, in more psychoanalytical terms, as an explicit rejection of his exiled father. However, greater consideration might also be given to the huge expansion of theatrical activity that emerged in the wake of the Bolshevik Revolution. As one critic pointed out in 1919,

> It is hardly possible to point to any other epoch when the theatre would have occupied such an exceptionally great place in people's lives, would have become such an essential part of popular culture as now in Russia. Everywhere, throughout the length and breadth of the Republic, there is an insatiable thirst for the theatre and for its stirring impressions, and this thirst is not only not diminishing, but is steadily gaining strength. Theatre has become a necessity for everyone.[21]

Nor was the fact that this great expansion of theatrical activity took place under the most trying social conditions lost to contemporary commentators. Thus *Vestnik Teatr* (Theatre Bulletin) prophetically announced that same year that 'The future historian will record how throughout one of the bloodiest and most brutal of revolutions all of Russia was acting.'[22] This was perhaps not as eccentric a notion as it might initially appear to be. One of the major problems faced by the new regime was communicating its message to the masses it claimed to represent. In a nation in which illiteracy was a major obstacle to the dissemination of information, the power of performance to spread the spoken word took on a heightened significance. For example, many of the early public rallies at which both Lenin and Trotsky spoke had a distinctly theatrical dimension, the leaders proclaiming their ideas from hastily erected and improvised stages to eager audiences perhaps as curious about the spectacle being performed as the message being conveyed. The fact that these events were regularly photographed and filmed added to their essentially performative nature, not least as these two media were incapable at the time of conveying a verbal message. More importantly, as theatrical performances potentially secured large gatherings, they rapidly became the perfect arena for political discourse. As Rudnitsky has argued, early Soviet theatre was valued highly for its potential as 'a platform for political agitation' with many performances accompanied by political speeches.[23] To expand further the propaganda potential of this means of mass communication, a whole host of new amateur theatre troupes was formed, including the Blue Blouse Theatre Troupes, which toured the countryside performing what became known as agit-plays.[24] Explicitly political in both content and function, these early Bolshevik performances were specifically intended to educate and transform the new audiences of workers and peasants.

By 1920, the Red Army alone could boast a highly impressive 2,000 troupes, stationed throughout Soviet-occupied territory. Many of these, like Eisenstein's Corps of Engineers troupe, staged their productions in abandoned schools or farm buildings in remote regions. Here, conditions necessarily demanded a high degree of improvisation. The productions themselves were often highly simplistic and direct in their narratives and staging, and presented a clear propagandistic message frequently contrasting the caricatured pre-Revolutionary exploitative bourgeois with the heroic new Bolshevik worker. A crucial source for this style was Mayakovsky's production of *Mystery-Bouffe*, staged by Meyerkhold in Petrograd on the first anniversary of the Bolshevik Revolution. Designated by Lunacharsky as 'placard-style' theatre, these early agit-plays drew on a whole host of popular cultural forms familiar to their new audiences, from street slogans and newspaper head-lines to mystery plays and circus performances. All this was to leave its indelible mark on Eisenstein's early forays into theatre and, indeed, on his cinematic work.

Eisenstein's first professional engagement in the world of theatre, working for Yeliseyev in the spring of 1920, was certainly a major break for the young designer. However, the first few months of his new career were perhaps not as auspicious as he had hoped they might be. No sooner had he joined than the troupe was incorporated into a broader umbrella organization known as PUZAP (Political Administration of the Western Front) and sent to Smolensk. Here, Eisenstein was to discover that all theatrical activi-ty had been temporarily suspended, as a consequence of which he spent several months sitting around with little to do. When PUZAP was transferred to Minsk shortly after the Bolshevik defeat of the Poles, Eisenstein participated in the decoration of an agit-train, but gained little other theatrical experience. By October of the same year, with the Civil War grinding to a halt, he, along with countless other Red Army draftees, was demobilized. His early opportunity to make his mark as a Soviet artist had largely come to nought.

In the autumn of 1920, Eisenstein, together with his fellow soldiers Pavel Arensky and Leonid Nikitin, set off for Moscow to study Japanese in the Oriental Languages Department of the Red

Army General Staff Academy. Having heard about the course through Arensky, Eisenstein, as a gifted linguist, was keen to sign up. He was also inspired by his new-found interest in Japanese culture, in particular kabuki theatre, as well as the opportunity to move to the new capital of the Soviet Union, home to some of the most exciting and adventurous theatrical experiments of the period. Other more immediate concerns may also have been at the forefront of Eisenstein's mind, such as the regular food rations offered to General Staff Academy students at a time of continuing shortages. Whatever the main inspiration, Moscow was to remain his home until his death.

Once in the capital, Eisenstein's career moved rapidly forward, whether as a consequence of good fortune or of judiciously selected contacts. Within a few weeks of his arrival he was introduced to the director Valentin Smyshlyaev and, despite his limited professional experience, invited to act as set and costume designer for the Proletkult Theatre. The more experimental ideas of this radical organization chimed well with Eisenstein's own emerging, revolutionary approach to theatre production, even if his class origins were sometimes a cause for concern. Over the next five years, he cut his creative teeth working for Proletkult, participating in a host of influential and controversial productions including *The Mexican* (1921); *Enough Simplicity for Every Wise Man* (1923), subsequently known as *Wise Man*; *Do You Hear Me, Moscow?* (1923); and *Gas Masks* (1924).

Towards the end of 1920 Smyshlyaev joined forces with the writer Boris Arvatov to produce a play on a Revolutionary theme for Proletkult. For source material they turned to a short story by the American writer Jack London titled 'The Mexican' (1911). London's adventure stories had proved highly popular in the early Bolshevik period with many of his books translated into Russian. In all probability, it was the American author's frequent emphasis on the underdog who valiantly fights oppression to overcome adversity by a combination of physical endurance and sheer willpower that spoke directly to Bolshevik experience. London's socialist sympathies certainly didn't hurt. On completion of the script, Smyshlyaev secured the agreement of the Proletkult Theatre to stage the play and engaged Eisenstein, together with Nikitin, to design the sets and costumes. This break proved to be more than timely for Eisenstein. Shortly after gaining the commission, he was forced to leave the General Staff Academy, as he was no longer in the army. With his stipend and food ration withdrawn, he needed the limited income offered by Proletkult. Freed from his other responsibilities, Eisenstein poured all his energies into the theatre.

The Mexican proved to be a highly topical subject for a Proletkult agit-play. London's narrative recounts the exploits of Felipe Rivera, a diminutive but resilient street kid who turns to prize-fighting to finance the Mexican revolutionary party on the eve of the 1910 overthrow of the corrupt Porfirio Diaz. Rivera, here a metaphor for the exploited Mexican workers, is pitched against a highly trained and, unlike Rivera himself, well-nourished American fighter called Danny Ward. Predictably, Rivera defeats the champion, thus earning enough money to buy guns for the revolutionaries about to launch their insurgency. On this level, the Smyshlyaev/Arvatov script conformed largely to conventional agit-plays of the time. The emphasis on boxing as revolutionary action also carried intriguing connotations in the context of the early Soviet period. Introduced into Russia in the late nineteenth century, boxing had rapidly acquired a popular following, particularly among working-class audiences. In 1918, for example, amid the turmoil of the Civil War, the city of Moscow staged major boxing competitions which drew huge crowds.[25] For some, boxing was the quintessential proletarian sport, not least as it was typically staged in music halls, circuses and fairgrounds, regarded as proletarian venues. In 1920, however, voices were raised in opposition to the sport, described as the exploitation of working-class fighters simply to entertain the wealthy. In this context, *The Mexican* was always likely to prove a topical, even controversial, production. Eisenstein's contribution to its staging further exacerbated this tension.

For Smyshlyaev, a student of Stanislavsky, the significance of *The Mexican* lay in its psychological study of Rivera, the young boxer who hardly ever spoke and who was described by London as 'the Revolution incarnate . . . the flame and the spirit of it, the insatiable cry for vengeance that makes no cry but that slays noiselessly.'[26] Thus Rivera appeared as a cipher for the worker-hero responsible for bringing about the October Revolution. Given the sombre mood of London's tale, Smyshlyaev was probably unprepared for the costume solutions proposed by Eisenstein and Nikitin. For example, the boxing managers, signifying capitalist exploitation, were dressed in lurid checked and striped suits reminiscent of circus-clown outfits. To distinguish the manager of the champion from that of Rivera, one costume was designed to emphasize squares, the other spheres, each actor donning a mask based upon these geometrical forms. Other characters, such as a news reporter, wore equally bizarre costumes adorned with slogans and sported large red noses. The sets, too, consisted of abstract geometrical forms clearly derived from the Cubist-inspired designs popularized in Alexander Tairov's Kamerny Theatre.

Eisenstein's deployment of a circus aesthetic in his first major production doubtless reflected his childhood fascination with clowns and popular entertainment. However, this caricatured presentation of character and setting was hardly a radical gesture in the early 1920s. As has been seen, the circus had been eagerly embraced by the new regime as a form of popular culture likely to entice newly enfranchised audiences. Indeed, the presence of the recently formed International Union of Circus Artists at the parade to celebrate the first anniversary of the October Revolution had marked the growing significance of the circus within early Soviet culture.[27] Many early Soviet theatre directors also embraced the circus aesthetic. In 1919, for example, Yuri Annenkov introduced both clowns and acrobats into his production of Tolstoy's *The First Distiller* (1886) at the Hermitage Theatre in Petrograd while Sergei Radlov recruited professional circus performers, including jugglers and trapeze artists, to perform in his Folk Comedy Theatre productions. Eisenstein's deployment of circus costumes and performances in *The Mexican* should be seen in this context.

However, he was far from simply jumping on the bandwagon. The most significant innovation in the production, usually ascribed to him, comes in the third act, in which the fight between Rivera and Ward takes place. Smyshlyaev originally proposed that this action should take place offstage, with the onstage actors playing fight spectators. Instead, Eisenstein advocated that a real boxing ring be set up in the middle of the auditorium and a real fight staged. Eisenstein later put great emphasis on the importance of 'real fighting, bodies crashing to the ring floor, panting, the shine of sweat on torsos and finally, the unforgettable smacking of gloves against taut skin and strained muscles.'[28] Given the artificiality of the circus-style costumes and settings, this more realist, even gritty, presentation certainly highlighted the metaphorical significance of the fight itself as both the key turning point in the narrative and a signifier of the Bolshevik Revolution. At the same time, this staging raised equally vital questions about the nature of boxing for contemporary audiences, not least of which concerned the role of the spectator. As boxing was most commonly staged within music hall and circus venues, here the setting was entirely appropriate. However, both the actors on stage and the audience would represent the fight spectators, actors and audience thus effectively becoming one and the same. By turning the audience into spectators at a notionally real boxing match, the ambiguous status of boxing – popular proletarian spectator sport or signifier of capitalist exploitation – was brought to the fore. In the end, fire marshals prevented Eisenstein from placing the ring exactly where he wanted it. Undaunted, he managed to bring it downstage and closer to the audience, thus distinguishing the two forms of action within the play.

Eisenstein's contribution to *The Mexican* brought him both acclaim and, in the short term, a small improvement in his finances. Bigger changes, occasioned by the end of the Civil War, would now have an impact on his fledgling career. In March 1921, the upper echelons of the Communist Party were gathering at the Tenth Party Congress to discuss a major policy shift. Lenin declared it time to make the transition from War Communism to the NEP (New Economic Policy). Perceived by many as a political step backwards, NEP reintroduced a market economy as a temporary stage to help rebuild a nation devastated by conflict. One immediate impact in cultural circles was that many of those organizations that had benefited from extensive state support had their subsidies drastically reduced, or even removed entirely. For the time being they would have by generate their own income.

Initially, Proletkult remained relatively unaffected, protected by its large membership subscriptions. However, Lenin's constant attacks on the organization, which he feared was seeking too much independence from the state, had a serious impact on its wider reputation. To make matters worse, Eisenstein's relationship with Smyshlyaev, who was never fully comfortable with the young designer's experimental approach, was deteriorating rapidly. Between 1921 and 1923, Eisenstein continued to work as designer for several Proletkult productions, though few had anything like the impact of *The Mexican*. In the late summer of 1921 his career took yet another important turn, however, when he enrolled at the newly formed GVYRM (State Higher Directors' Workshop), where he would spend a year studying under Meyerkhold, whom he had admired for so long.

Following the Bolshevik Revolution, Meyerkhold was among the first in the theatrical community to support the new regime. In

Sergei Eisenstein, photographed when working for the Proletkult Theatre, Moscow, 1922.

1918 he joined the Bolshevik Party, rapidly becoming one of the most important directors in the Soviet Union, holding an influential position within Narkompros. Over the next few years he explored the possibilities for a new, post-Revolutionary theatre and was responsible for some of the most innovative productions of the early Soviet period. He remains best known for his interests in Pavlovian reflexology and his development of biomechanics, a training programme designed to encourage actors to engage simultaneously with mind and body. When, in 1921 Meyerkhold launched GVYRM as a base from which he could disseminate his theories regarding stagecraft, Eisenstein proved to be one of the major beneficiaries.

As GVYRM offered no financial support, Eisenstein continued to work during his studies. Along with Sergei Yutkevich, a fellow student and, later, an influential film designer and director, he produced set and costume designs for MastFor, the theatre workshop run by Nikolai Foregger, also famous for his promotion of both music-hall and circus performance, as well as continuing to work for Proletkult. Among the productions Eisenstein and Yutkevich worked on at this time were *A Humane Attitude to Horses*, *The Kidnapper* and *Macbeth*. In mid-1922, Eisenstein and Yutkevich accompanied Foregger's troupe on a trip to Petrograd, where they met the young Grigory Kozintsev and Leonid Trauberg, who had recently founded FEKS (Factory of the Eccentric Actor). Like many of their contemporaries, Kozintsev and Trauberg embraced contemporary popular culture, including music-hall and circus performance. To this heady mix they added poster art and the cinema. Kozintsev and Trauberg were great admirers of American film, especially of Charlie Chaplin, whose mechanistically inspired gymnastic movements brought together circus acrobatics and socially conscious narratives. In a famous diatribe published in Petrograd in 1922, Kozintsev and Trauberg provocatively declared, 'We prefer Charlie's arse to Eleanora Duse's hands,' thereby, in one fell swoop, prioritizing America over Europe, film over stage, and artifice over naturalism.[29] More significantly, they practised what they preached; in their first stage production, *The Marriage* (1922) they introduced projected film alongside slapstick sequences, jazz songs and acrobatic tricks. The impact this mix had on Eisenstein would be evident in his first production as director for Proletkult staged the following year, *Wise Man*.

Eisenstein's year at GVYRM was by far the most productive of his early career so far. In addition to the extracurricular activities already mentioned, he designed a stage set for Meyerkhold's proposed, though never staged, production of George Bernard Shaw's *Heartbreak House*. Here the emphasis on stark, geometrical forms linked with wire and rope to produce a mechanistic structure reminiscent of circus equipment (trapezes, tightropes etc.) showed the strong influence of the Constructivists Lyubov Popova and Varvara Stepanova, both of whom worked on Meyerkhold's two most influential stage productions of this period, *The Magnanimous Cuckold* and *The Death of Tarelkin*.

Eisenstein's frequently stormy relationship with Meyerkhold led to a break in the autumn of 1922. Although they had been extremely close, Eisenstein's activities beyond GVYRM were clearly a cause of tension, with Meyerkhold reputedly accusing him of betrayal, more specifically of sharing his innovations with MastFor and Proletkult. As tensions increased, Eisenstein was gradually forced out of the school. Despite this, he would later write, 'I never loved, adored or worshipped anyone as I did my teacher.'[30] Shortly before his departure from GVYRM, he accepted a position as artistic director for a troupe of travelling performers at Proletkult. This would provide him with the opportunity to take full control of a production for the first time.

In 1923, Lunacharsky launched a campaign calling upon theatre directors to stage the plays of Alexander Ostrovsky, the nineteenth-century playwright famous for his comedies satirizing the Moscow merchant classes. Although conceived ostensibly to celebrate the centenary of Ostrovsky's birth, the campaign also set out to reinforce the policy that post-Revolutionary culture should draw upon the legacy of the Russian classics. Meyerkhold immediately responded by staging *A Profitable Post*, a relatively conventional production compared with his recent output. He also began work on a more experimental production of *The Forest*, to be staged the following year.[31] Tairov similarly introduced Ostrovsky's *The Storm* into the Kamerny Theatre repertoire, while Stanislavsky staged *A Passionate Heart* at the Moscow Arts Theatre.

Doubtless aware of Meyerkhold's plans, Eisenstein similarly turned to Ostrovsky. His production of *Wise Man* was, without doubt, the most radical reinterpretation of the latter's works to hit the Moscow stage. It was also, one imagines, far from what Lunacharsky had in mind. Drawing extensively on his recent experiences with Meyerkhold, Foregger and FEKS, Eisenstein presented a carnivalesque pageant of circus tricks, stunts, songs, jokes and outlandish spectacles; the stage had a round playing area, a striped

Production photograph from *Enough Simplicity for Every Wise Man*, Proletkult Theatre, Moscow, 1923.

canvas backdrop and a tightrope suspended above the audience's heads. Sergei Tretyakov, the Futurist poet and playwright, was recruited to rewrite the script entirely, in the process transforming Ostrovsky's characters into clowns, acrobats and thinly veiled caricatures of contemporary political figures. As with *The Mexican*, references to the circus were deployed both to reinforce the narrative and to convey a pro-Bolshevik political message.

Ostrovsky's original play satirizes the arrogance and pomposity of merchants who are easily duped by the lies and flattery of the main character, Glumov. Eisenstein, in contrast, transported the setting to a contemporary Paris inhabited by Russian émigrés, representing the flotsam and jetsam of the pre-Revolutionary era. He also presented one of these characters, Golutvin – played by his friend and, later, collaborator Grigory Alexandrov – as an NEP man, an exploiter of the newly reintroduced market economy. Thus the corruption that characterized the Tsarist epoch was simultaneously seen as the past, now safely exiled, and the present, still a threat. When Alexandrov performed the most famous stunt from the production, making an entrance by walking down a tightrope stretched across the entire auditorium, he therefore metaphorically highlighted both the precariousness and the guile of the former bourgeoisie with the rope itself signifying the tenuous, but still existent, links between Paris and Moscow, past and present, corruption and honesty. Notably, Eisenstein also introduced a priest, a rabbi and a mullah among this degraded class of characters, thus directly addressing the official state demand that theatre be deployed as part of a wider anti-religious campaign.

Wise Man caused a stir among the critics. However, many highlighted the sheer complexity of the references as highly problematic, arguing that the play was largely unintelligible to the majority of spectators. While audiences may indeed have enjoyed the spectacle, the political message, it was argued, risked being buried too deeply to be effective. To counter this limitation, each

Glumov's Diary (filmed sequence included in *Enough Simplicity for Every Wise Man*, Proletkult Theatre, Moscow, 1923).

production was preceded by Tretyakov appearing on stage to explain both the content and the meaning of the play, a tacit acknowledgement that the critics were right. Lest even this prove ineffectual, the programme carried a description of the action.[32]

Although *Wise Man* marked a major contribution to early Soviet theatre, its reputation, at least as far as Eisenstein's future career was concerned, has perhaps come to depend more upon the fact that it was during this production that he first picked up a movie camera. He incorporated several short film sequences into the production, each projected onto a large screen at the back of the stage, while the performance concluded with a five-minute filmic epilogue subsequently dubbed *Glumov's Diary*. While the inclusion of film sequences was clearly inspired by Kozintsev and Trauberg's *The Marriage*, it also served to reinforce the centrality of the circus aesthetic. After all, cinema had started its career in Russia as a spectacle popularly displayed at fairgrounds and in music halls. As far as Ostrovsky's original play was concerned, the use of film to represent Glumov's diary was also entirely appropriate. Within the narrative, the diary represents Glumov's true, unadorned opinion of the main characters, in contrast to the flattery and deceit he presents to their faces. Thus, by turning his diary into a film, Eisenstein was alluding to the widely held assumption that cinema potentially offered a truthful, documentary vision of Soviet life. To emphasize this notion further, he shot and edited the sequence to resemble the Pathé and Gaumont newsreels that had dominated pre-Revolutionary cinema. At the same time *Glumov's Diary* offered a wry comment on the recently launched newsreels, presented under the title *Kino-Pravda* (Cinema Truth), made by Dziga Vertov.[33]

Yet *Glumov's Diary* also deliberately highlighted the tension between truth and fiction by including episodes reminiscent of Hollywood adventure films. For example, it shows a masked thief in full evening dress (a topos developed in early Harry Piel movies and developed further in the *Fantômas* series that had proven so popular in pre-Revolutionary Russia) climbing up a spire and jumping from a tall building. Through trick editing he is seen landing safely in a passing car and thence driven to the very theatre in which *Wise Man* was being played. Seconds after the filmed Glumov enters the theatre, the real Glumov (or the actor playing him) leaps onstage carrying a reel of film representing the diary. Thus, film and theatrical performance, the documentary and the dramatic, overlap, and the audience is never quite clear what is truth and what is fiction. To highlight further this coexistence of reality and contrivance, Eisenstein also deployed dissolve editing in *Glumov's Diary*. Glumov's capacity for deceit is revealed when he is shown performing an acrobatic tumble before each of the main characters, only to be transformed into the object of their desire; a cannon for one character, a donkey for another, an adorable child for a third. As a political comment, Eisenstein defined one charac-

Production photograph from *Do You Hear Me, Moscow?*, 1923.

ter's desire as a swastika, a heavily loaded reference in light of
the recent rise in popularity of Hitler's National Socialist Party
in Germany.

These filmic devices were highly conventional and familiar to
contemporary audiences in the early 1920s. For Eisenstein, however,
the film medium now suggested a range of creative possibilities
that stretched beyond the potential of live theatre. Over the following
year he produced two more theatre productions in which he was
already beginning to think beyond the confines of the stage. In the
late summer of 1923, he began work on a new play titled *Do You
Hear Me, Moscow?* Described by its author, Tretyakov once more,
as an 'agit-guignol', the play again deployed both circus costumes
and acrobatic movements. Its political references, however, were
far more overtly displayed. Set in contemporary Germany, *Do You
Hear Me, Moscow?* tells the story of a group of exploited workers
who rebel against their oppressors to bring about a political revolu-

tion.[34] With the former openly identified as Communists and the latter as Fascists, the play directly addressed the political situation in Germany, where the Communist Party, the KPD, was clashing with Hitler's National Socialists amid the chaos of hyper-inflation. In true Proletkult fashion, the main characters were loosely sketched, representing the stereotypes of heroic socialist worker or evil capitalist. The main theme of the play, however, was the importance of cultural transformation to revolutionary action, a subject dear to the hearts of all Proletkultists.

Here, the stage set played a major role in the narrative. In the first act, the audience is presented with a new, yet to be unveiled monument situated at the back of the stage. This, we are informed, represents the historical figure of the Iron Count, infamous for his subjugation of the local population and exploitation of their labour. The monument is the work of the artist Grubbe, who, together with the poet Grabbe, is represented as a fawning lackey constantly striving to ingratiate himself with the present Count in an attempt to secure further commissions. Here we have old art, whose sole purpose is to flatter the wealthy. However, in the final scene, when the monument is uncovered, it has been replaced with a huge, poster-like portrait of Lenin before which the revolutionaries unfurl a banner declaiming 'All Power to the Soviets'. It is the workers themselves who have replaced the Iron Count with the People's Hero, and thus the new art is not the work of the individual but of the masses. To reinforce the centrality of cultural revolution, the uprising takes place during a pageant at which the old regime recites badly written epic poetry. The workers, performing a mime as part of the pageant, have secretly replaced stage rifles with real weapons which they subsequently use to launch their revolution. Here the mass procession so beloved of Proletkult becomes simultaneously the means of the revolution and its re-enactment. This denouement thus reinforces the notion that culture must be transformed for revolution to be successful.

Significantly, the play was first performed on 7 November 1923, to mark the sixth anniversary of the Bolshevik Revolution. When, the very next day, Hitler launched his abortive Beer Hall Putsch in Munich, the political resonances of *Do You Hear Me, Moscow?* were surely felt throughout the Soviet capital.

Eisenstein's staging of *Do You Hear Me, Moscow?* notably contrasted the circus costumes worn by the old regime with workers' outfits that bore more than a passing resemblance to Popova's *prozodezhda*, or production clothing, deployed in Meyerkhold's *The Magnanimous Cuckold*. Moreover, Tretyakov's stage instructions – 'mime members use stylized plastic-ballet methods' – further suggests that both he and Eisenstein intended to deploy Meyerkholdian biomechanics as a means to distinguish the workers from the bourgeoisie. In this way *Do You Hear Me, Moscow?* might usefully be read as a development of *Wise Man*, in which Eisenstein once again emphasized the circus aesthetic so popular in early 1920s theatre. However, this stylization was now more explicitly mapped onto a conventional melodrama format with an easily definable political message. When the cast, at the very end of the play, called to the audience, 'Do you hear me, Moscow?' and prompted the response, 'I do', few, one senses, left the theatre unaware of the production's political significance.

The collaboration of Eisenstein and Tretyakov on *Wise Man* and *Do You Hear Me, Moscow?* usefully reflects one of the key tensions within Proletkult practices at this time. On the one hand, Eisenstein prioritized spectacle as a means to entice the audience. In this way he extolled the virtues of new cultural forms strongly associated with the proletarian classes as well as the importance of theatre as a means of popular diversion. Tretyakov, on the other hand, emphasized a clearly definable narrative, even if drawing upon conventional bourgeois melodrama, as a means to inculcate class consciousness in the spectator. Here the emphasis is far more on didacticism. Yet both sought directly to shape the audience's thinking processes. With their next, and final, collaboration, the pendulum swung far more in the direction of Tretyakov.

The play *Gas Masks* is loosely based on an incident reported in *Pravda*. Following an explosion at a gas factory, a group of workers set out to effect a repair and thus save the factory.[35] However, there are no gas masks available as the director has squandered the money put aside for such safety equipment. As the factory is no longer in private hands, the workers set out to save this vital enterprise, each individual risking gas poisoning by working for short periods without protection. To heighten the drama, one of the workers, Petya, is the son of the negligent director and suffers from a weak heart. Against advice, he insists on taking his turn in the poisoned gas shaft, thus showing his rejection of the past and commitment to the new regime. Tragically, the strain is too much, and he collapses and dies. Only then is it discovered that the director's secretary has secretly married him and is carrying his child. The director, showing both remorse and self-pity, requests that the child be named Petya in honour of his heroic father. The secretary, however, insists on naming the child 'Protivogaz' (literally, 'Gas Mask').[36] Here, industry and collectivity are notably prioritized over individualism and family ties.

Written towards the end of 1923, rehearsals for *Gas Masks* began in January of the following year. By the time of its first performance on 29 February, the martyrology of Petya had taken on a new dimension. Just one month earlier, approximately half a million mourners had endured long waits in the bitter cold to file past the recently deceased Lenin as he lay in state in Moscow's Hall of Columns.[37]

The staging of *Gas Masks* was striking, to say the least, and reflected Eisenstein's growing concerns regarding the limitations of the theatre. Once again, however, the influence of his former teacher could be felt. The previous year, Meyerkhold had staged a one-off performance of *The Earth in Turmoil* in a factory in Kiev, before bringing the production to the Moscow stage; the play also notably included a heroic death scene.[38] Eisenstein, however, proposed to take this idea one step further by using a real factory as the setting for all performances. Having gained the agreement of the Moscow Gas Factory situated on the outskirts of the city, he erected a small wooden platform in front of the giant turbo-generators on the factory floor. Before this he placed audience seating consisting of wooden planks laid across stacks of bricks. The actors wore real workers' overalls and no make-up, and used factory tools as props. Both the sounds and the smell of the factory setting were integral aspects of the production, and, as a final touch of authenticity, the play was scheduled to conclude with the precise moment when the night shift arrived for work, thus breaking down the distinction between staged action and real labour.

As a spectacle *Gas Masks* struggled to find an audience and lasted only four performances, some of them sparsely attended. Critical reception was also muted. Yet the production marked a significant shift in Eisenstein's work. The eccentric clown costumes and gestures that had made *Wise Man* and *Do You Hear Me, Moscow?* such spectacles now gave way to a greater sense of naturalism and a heightened political message. However, the emphasis on acrobatics was not abandoned, but rather transformed into the carefully orchestrated movements of the worker-actors. Thus one critic complained about the latter's 'deliberately angular movement' and an excessive emphasis on gymnastics.[39] This more mediated influence of the circus aesthetic would come to the fore in much of Eisenstein's early film work.

Between 1920 and 1924, Eisenstein's tenure at Proletkult, along with his education under Meyerkhold, had prepared him for a career as an innovative stage director. Throughout the rest of his career he would draw heavily upon the experiences he gained during this highly experimental period. But, for now, the theatre was no longer to be his milieu. Moving off the stage had opened a world of possibilities, and it was as a filmmaker that Eisenstein would develop these most effectively.

2
Consolidation

The resounding failure of *Gas Masks* might have proven a major setback to a lesser mortal than Eisenstein. Yet, from the ashes of this debacle he rapidly rose, phoenix-like, to consolidate his reputation as a major player in Soviet cultural politics. Within just over a year he had completed *Strike* and secured the single most important film commission of the early Bolshevik period: to produce a movie to commemorate the twentieth anniversary of the 1905 Revolution. The product of this commission, *Battleship Potemkin*, was soon distributed around the world and brought Eisenstein international fame. By early 1927, less than three years since *Gas Masks*, 'the boy from Riga' was being lauded, both at home and abroad, as one of the greatest filmmakers of all time.[1]

Eisenstein's early theoretical writings also made a significant contribution towards consolidating his reputation. In 1923, he had published a short article in the influential cultural journal '*Left Front of the Arts*'. 'The Montage of Attractions', written as both a response to, and analysis of, *Wise Man*, effectively outlined Eisenstein's theoretical approach to theatre work. It would also form the basis for his early experiments in cinematography. Here, in true Proletkult style, he clarified his cultural mission as no less than 'the moulding of the audience in a desired direction'.[2] To achieve this, he advocated a new method in which the presentation of key moments, or attractions, would serve collectively to direct the audience's response. For Eisenstein, an attraction constituted 'any aggressive moment . . . that subjects the audience to emotional or psychological influence'.[3] These could be as seemingly obscure as 'the colour of the prima donna's tights' or as intrusive as 'a salvo under the seats of the auditorium'.[4] The director's role, in effect, was to orchestrate and choreograph these 'attractions' in such a manner as to determine an audience's reactions precisely. Notably, Eisenstein claimed that this could be achieved scientifically, the bringing together ('montage') of such 'attractions' thus being 'mathematically calculated to produce specific emotional shocks in the spectator in their proper order within the whole'.[5] And it was this 'montage', Eisenstein further claimed, that provided 'the only opportunity of perceiving the ideological aspect of what is being shown, the final ideological conclusion.'[6]

Eisenstein was here drawing upon the Pavlovian concept of conditioned reflexes, thus pursuing ideas that Meyerkhold had also been exploring in his experiments in biomechanics. The ultimate question, however, was to what extent Eisenstein's 'montage of attractions' could actually mould audience response? As things turned out, early Soviet audiences were far less malleable that Pavlov's salivating dogs and responded to Eisenstein's work in ways less consistent than he would perhaps have wished. In 1923, however, much of this remained to be tested. While the Proletkult theatre had offered ample opportunities for Eisenstein to try out his theories, the experience of staging *Gas Masks* in a real factory had opened up a new set of possibilities. Rather than return to the limitations of the stage, cinema now seemed to offer greater potential, not least for exploring the new possibilities of montage.

Eisenstein's move from theatre to cinema could not have come at a more propitious time. With the Civil War concluded and NEP beginning to take effect, the new regime began to divert more of its time, energy and resources to the field of culture and, more specifically, the reorganization of the cinema industry. Prior to the Revolution, Russian cinema had depended upon private commercial investment. After 1917, however, the instability brought about by the Civil War forced many of these pre-Revolutionary enterprises to abandon the country, thus leaving both a financial and a technical vacuum. Consequently, with relatively few new productions to screen, the curtain was increasingly brought down on many cinemas throughout the former Empire. Despite this decline, the new regime valued cinema as a medium of propaganda and thus turned its hand to the production of short agitational films, or *agitki*. These films, like the Red Army agit-plays in which Eisenstein had participated, were explicitly political in nature and designed to inculcate Bolshevik values. Screened throughout the nation in makeshift cinemas with portable projection equipment, or in agit-trains that roamed the rural expanses, these films were aimed largely at illiterate audiences who had not otherwise been exposed to Bolshevik ideas. Yet, the new regime clearly had a battle on its hands. As it turned out, audiences consistently preferred the melodramas and spectacles that had characterized pre-Revolutionary Russian cinema.

In the autumn of 1919, the Soviet government made its first major intervention into cinema matters by nationalizing the industry. Yet, with continuing shortages of both personnel and equipment, much of which had previously been imported from the West, this decree was characterized far more by aspiration than by practical activity. Indeed, many condemned the government for dragging its heels and failing to support the industry's development. The death of Lenin in January 1924 was also to make a notable contribution to the development of early Soviet cinema. In the wake of this cataclysmic event, a veritable cult of Lenin emerged. As a part of this focus on his legacy, countless authors published books and articles recounting his life or conversations and meetings in which he had participated. In this context Lenin's copious writings and proclamations gradually took on the mantle of quasi-Holy Scripture. Among the Lenin memorial literature was a volume edited by Grigory Boltyansky, *Lenin and Cinema* (1925), which included an article by Lunacharsky titled 'Conversation with Lenin'. This article is best remembered today for Lunacharsky's claimed verbatim recollection of Lenin's saying that 'of all the arts for us the most important is cinema'.[7] This famous phrase would soon become a clarion call for Soviet filmmakers. Eisenstein himself would frequently make recourse to Lenin's support for cinema as a justification for his own activities in the many speeches and declarations he would make throughout his working life.

Perhaps more importantly, Lunacharsky also reiterated Lenin's notion, previously outlined in an article published in 1922, that the Soviet state should encourage the production of both documentary films, in the form of newsreels, and entertainment movies. Betraying his personal preference for drama, Lunacharsky thus recalled, 'Vladimir Ilyich considered it no less, but on the contrary even more, important that there should be artistic propaganda for our ideas in the form of entertainment films, depicting fragments of life and permeated with our ideas.'[8] By highlighting a distinction between documentary newsreels and the dramatic feature film, Lunacharsky was self-consciously drawing attention to an issue that was already beginning to divide the burgeoning Soviet cinema industry into two camps.[9]

On one side of the divide lay the school of Dziga Vertov and the Cine-Eyes, or *kinoki*, who effectively rejected all forms of film drama. For this group any acted production was reflective of pre-Revolutionary bourgeois culture. In a manifesto published in 1922, Vertov pronounced 'the old films, the romantic, the theatricalized, etc, to be leprous'.[10] Expanding the metaphor of disease, he further warned audiences away from such productions in the following – though, it might be added, overtly dramatic – manner: 'Don't come near! Don't look! Mortally dangerous! Contagious!'[11] Such film dramas, the *kinoki* believed, should be replaced with a new cinema based exclusively on documentary footage revealing, to quote a famous Vertov phrase, 'life caught unawares'. Vertov valued many of the cinematic techniques that had been developed in Hollywood, not least the emphasis on what he referred to as 'ostentatious dynamism' generated by 'rapid shot changes and close-ups', essentially the early development of cinematic montage. Yet these techniques, he argued, needed to be deployed more scientifically, as a means to expose and celebrate the new Soviet citizen: the worker at his lathe, the peasant on his tractor, the driver in his engine.[12] Vertov's notion that the fundamental purpose of Soviet cinema was to inspire the masses and effect change in their political consciousness chimed well with Eisenstein's developing views. His rejection of 'so-called fiction film', however, would set the two directors at odds.

On the other side of the divide lay more conventional film dramas, though these might also be subdivided into two categories. The first included the plethora of imported films, whether American or European, that dominated the cinemas not only of Moscow and Leningrad but also of the further reaches of the Soviet Union.[13] Indeed, the implementation of the profit-driven NEP in 1921 effectively opened the floodgates to foreign films. As Denise Youngblood has shown, throughout the early 1920s foreign productions constituted a significantly higher percentage of new releases than Soviet movies.[14] Moreover, Western stars, including Chaplin, Douglas Fairbanks, Mary Pickford, Pola Negri, Harry Piel and Conrad Veidt, soon became household names. The second category of film drama constituted home-grown movies, although these did not begin to appear in any numbers until the early to mid-1920s. In 1923, for example, the first significant feature films addressing Revolutionary subject matter began to appear. These included *Brigade Commander Ivanov* and *The Little Red Devils*, both based on Civil War subjects.

The year 1924 proved to be a major turning point in Soviet film production. The fledgling enterprise Goskino, formed in December

1922, was replaced with a bigger and better funded organization, Sovkino. To match the new level of ambition, 76 new films were produced, nearly three times the output of the previous year and more than the previous three years combined.[15] It was not just the volume of production that had changed, however. Two films released that year, Yakov Protazanov's *Aelita* and Lev Kuleshov's *The Extraordinary Adventures of Mr West in the Land of the Bolsheviks*, were widely regarded as marking a qualitative shift in Soviet production.[16] Notably, both of these movies embraced, even celebrated, the Hollywood genres of comedy, adventure and romantic melodrama. At the same time, they introduced specifically Soviet themes into their plots. The release of both *Aelita* and *Mr West* suggested that Soviet cinema had potentially come of age, showing a level of professional and technical expertise that augured well for the future.

It was against this background that Eisenstein made his entry into the movie business. As a relative novice, he recognized the need to expand his knowledge. His contacts in the avant-garde world soon afforded him an important opportunity. In March 1924, just a few weeks after the closure of *Gas Masks*, Eisenstein visited Esfir Shub, a literary graduate and partner to the Constructivist theorist Alexei Gan. At this time Shub held an important position within Goskino, working extensively in the editing room. Indeed, her mastery of editing techniques was evident later in her trilogy *The Fall of the Romanov Dynasty*, *The Great Way* and *Lev Tolstoy and the Russia of Nikolai II*, productions compiled and edited together from pre-Revolutionary archival footage. At Goskino, Shub was specifi- cally assigned to editing foreign films, thus effectively acting as censor, the nation's moral and political watchdog. Notably, the state did not seek to ban movies that did not conform to Soviet ideological principles; after all, the profit generated by foreign films was a major source of income. Rather, notionally dubious content was either edited out or re-edited. New inter-titles were then added to change, sometimes radically, the significance of a particular scene or even the whole narrative of the film. Eisenstein later offered an example of how this editing process operated:

> I cannot resist the pleasure of citing here one montage *tour de force* of this sort, executed by Boitler. One film bought from Germany was *Danton*, with Emil Jannings. As released on our screens, this scene was shown: Camille Desmoulins is condemned to the guillotine. Greatly agitated, Danton rushes to Robespierre, who turns aside and slowly wipes away a tear. The sub-title said, approximately, 'In the name of freedom, I had to sacrifice a friend . . . ' Fine.
>
> But who could have guessed that in the German original, Danton, represented as an idler, a petticoat-chaser, a splendid chap and the only positive figure in the midst of evil characters, that this Danton ran to the evil Robespierre and . . . spat in his face? And that it was this spit that Robespierre wiped from his face with a handkerchief? And that the title indicated Robespierre's hatred of Danton, a hate that in the end of the film motivates the condemnation of Jannings-Danton to the guillotine!
>
> Two tiny cuts had reversed the entire significance of this scene![17]

When Eisenstein visited Shub, she was working on a re-edited version of Fritz Lang's *Dr Mabuse, the Gambler* (1922), reducing the original two-part release, running at over four hours in length, to a single feature renamed *Gilded Rot*. Lang's tale of violent crime, gambling, hypnotism and the lurid tastes of the rich and powerful lent itself readily to a reconstruction as a quasi-political critique of Western decadence. Eisenstein reportedly helped with the rewriting of the inter-titles. Thus, it was through working with Shub that he gained his first exposure to the processes and, indeed, the enormous potential of film editing as a creative endeavour.

His next challenge was how to gain an opportunity to put this experience into practice and make his first film. In this new venture, his first port of call was his employer and head of the Moscow Proletkult, Valerian Pletnyov. Once again Eisenstein's timing was propitious. The previous year, Proletkult had launched its own cinematic enterprise, Proletkino, an organization that immediately set about attacking the new regime for its failure to produce specifically 'proletarian films'. Taking advantage of the moment, and fully aware of the budget limitations and potential egos involved, Eisenstein proposed that Pletnyov and he work together, the Proletkult leader producing the scripts and Eisenstein directing. Together they prepared an outline for an ambitious series of seven episodes recounting the rise of the working-class movement under the influence of the Bolshevik Party. This was to be titled *Towards the Dictatorship* and was to cover the period up to the October Revolution.[18] It soon became clear to Eisenstein, however, that Proletkino had insufficient funds to underwrite such a project. Undaunted, he approached Boris Mikhin, the director of Goskino, and gained permission to shoot a series of screen tests. According to the Formalist Viktor Shklovsky, the first two of these were rejected by Goskino, and, for a brief period, Eisenstein's career hung in the balance.[19] However, with the support of both Mikhin and the cameraman Edouard Tisse, who was later to work on all of Eisenstein's film productions, the young director was given another chance. As a consequence of this, on 1 April 1924, he signed an agreement to start work on a Proletkult–Goskino joint production. The result was *Strike*.

Although *Strike* constituted but one of the proposed seven episodes in the *Towards the Dictatorship* series, it was the only one to be completed. The film can best be categorized as a historical drama, in six reels, charting the events of an industrial dispute at a transport factory in pre-Revolutionary Russia. From the outset, *Strike* establishes a clear dialectical tension between two classes: the dispossessed workers and the egregiously exploitative bosses. As the plot unfolds, the workers gradually acquire consciousness of their own power and potential to bring about change. They organize a series of clandestine meetings, distribute illegal literature and form themselves into an organized mass, all this despite the best efforts of the bosses' lackeys and spies, who fail to thwart the workers' plans. Following the suicide of a worker unjustly accused of stealing an expensive piece of equipment, the workers unite to down tools and stage a walkout, bringing the factory to a standstill. The revolutionary moment having thus been enacted early in the plot, the movie turns its attention to the endurance demanded of the workers in sustaining the strike, and the efforts of agents provocateurs to break down worker unity. Nonetheless the bosses, having failed by various underhand ruses to break the workers' resolve, refuse to give in to the strikers' demands. Instead they send mounted soldiers into the workers' commune and perpetrate a massacre. The film ends with the camera panning over the dead bodies of the strikers, laid out as if in the aftermath of a military battle, and a subsequent close-up of the eyes of an angry worker staring directly out from the screen. With the aid of an inter-title, this anonymous individual extols the audience, as 'proletarians', to 'remember' such atrocities.

Even before its general release in April 1925, it was clear that *Strike* would have a significant impact in Soviet cultural circles. In mid-March it was positively reviewed in both the major press organs of the state, *Pravda* and *Izvestiya*, while the more specialist journal *Kinogazeta* hailed it as 'a major event for Soviet, Russian and world cinematography' and 'the first talented, original international and proletarian film'.[20] Eisenstein was even lauded as a Soviet D. W. Griffith.[21] Yet despite this heady praise, there was little consensus regarding the value of the film among the wider Soviet cinema community. Vertov, for example, perhaps unsurprisingly, condemned Eisenstein's use of actors and emphasis on melodrama.

Nor, it seems, was the public at large overly impressed. Despite its claimed status as the first original proletarian film, *Strike* failed to attract the very audience for whom it was notionally created, its run cut short in several cinemas to be replaced by the far more popular Hollywood drama *The Thief of Baghdad*, starring Douglas Fairbanks. Domestic reception, however, was not the only barometer of success or failure, and in the summer of 1925, *Strike* was awarded a gold medal at the 1925 *Exposition Internationale des Arts Décoratifs et Industriels Modernes* in Paris. This recognition was highly valued by the Soviet authorities, not least as it resulted in both the dissemination of Revolutionary ideas to a wider community and substantial income in hard currency.[22]

The final reel of *Strike* had barely reached the end of its spool at its Leningrad premiere when Eisenstein began work on two more film projects, both recounting episodes from the Civil War: *The Iron Flood*, based on Alexander Sefimovich's novel of the same name, and *Red Cavalry*, a proposed collaboration with the writer Isaak Babel. Both were soon abandoned, however. Eisenstein had parted company with Proletkult. After the release of *Strike* he became embroiled in an undignified wrangle with Pletnyov concerning his own authorship and financial rights, a dispute that resulted in his abandoning Proletkult or being sacked by Pletnyov, depending on whose version of events one believes.[23]

Much like *Strike*, Eisenstein's second movie started out as a significantly larger project. In March 1925 the state Jubilee Committee, established to oversee the commemoration of the twentieth anniversary of the 1905 Revolution, approached Eisenstein to make a film entitled *The Year 1905*. Together with Nina Agadzhanova-Shutko, screenwriter and member of the Bolshevik Party since 1907, he began work on a scenario, conceiving the film as a vast panorama of the events of 1905. These were to include, in six parts: the Russo–Japanese War; the massacre of innocent workers in St Petersburg, subsequently known as Bloody Sunday; popular

The 'Iron Five'
(left to right, Grigori
Alexandrov, Maxim
Straukh, Mikhail
Gomorov, Alexander
Antonov, Alexander
Levshin).

uprisings throughout city and countryside; a general strike and
its suppression by the state; counter-Revolutionary pogroms; and
the emergence of a political movement in the workers' district of
Krasnaya Presnya.[24] One small episode within this historical
overview would address the mutiny on the Russian naval vessel
Prince Potemkin. Eisenstein and Agadzhanova-Shutko continued
working on the scenario throughout the summer, holed up in a dacha
on the outskirts of Moscow. Under huge pressure to complete the
project within the calendar year, Eisenstein was still shooting in
Leningrad in late August 1925, assisted by his team known as the
'iron five': Grigory Alexandrov, Maxim Straukh, Mikhail Gomorov,
Alexander Antonov and Alexander Levshin. Bad light hampered

progress, however, and on the advice of Mikhail Kapchinsky, the by now highly anxious director of Goskino, they set off for Odessa to work under more advantageous conditions. It was there that the decision was taken to focus exclusively on the *Potemkin* mutiny. As Alexandrov would later point out, 'a single episode disposed of in three pages of an endless scenario' now became the whole film.[25]

Eisenstein's *Potemkin* recounts events on board the *Prince Potemkin* in June 1905. Initially, a rebellion is sparked off when sailors are offered rotten meat as food rations. Despite their protestation, the ship's medical officer declares the maggot-ridden rations fit for human consumption. When the sailors refuse to eat this offering, the captain raises the temperature by threatening to exact severe punishments. Although resistance, up to this point, has been passive, he threatens to execute some of the rebels, thus leading to a full-scale mutiny. During the ensuing melee, the sailors take control of the ship, throwing several of the officers overboard. Their victory celebration, however, is tempered by news of the death of Vakulinchuk, the leader of the mutineers, shot by one of the officers. His body is brought to rest in Odessa harbour, where it attracts the sympathy of the local population who come out in vast numbers to support the mutinous sailors. The crowd rapidly lines the docks and spills over onto the Richelieu steps, popularly known as the Odessa steps, connecting the city to the harbour. Fearful of this show of solidarity, the Tsarist authorities send armed troops to disperse the crowd, and, in one of world cinema's most famous scenes, the troops march, machine-like, down the Odessa steps, massacring hundreds of innocent citizens. Responding to this atrocity, the *Prince Potemkin* fires a salvo into the town, destroying the Generals' Headquarters. In the final sequence, the mutineers aboard the *Prince Potemkin* confront what appears to be the entire Black Sea Fleet. As they prepare to defend themselves, they call upon their fellow mariners to join them. In a tense, final moment

Exterior of the First Art Cinema, Moscow, for the premiere of *Battleship Potemkin*, January 1926.

the Russian navy relinquishes its opposition and joins the cause of the revolutionary sailors.

Like *Strike*, the release of *Potemkin* was widely promoted by the state. Following a grand preview at the Bolshoi Theatre, for which Eisenstein was reportedly still completing the editing of the final reel while the film was being screened, *Potemkin* premiered at the First Art Goskino Theatre in Moscow's Arbat district. To add to the prestige of the event, the front of the cinema was decorated with a three-dimensional model of the ship, complete with masts, flags and guns, while inside, the ushers were dressed in sailors' uniforms.[26] Critical responses were largely positive, perhaps the most euphoric being N. Volkhov's declaration in *Trud* that *Potemkin* signified 'the true victory of Soviet cinematography' and that the film constituted 'an authentic work of contemporary cinematographic art, deeply thrilling in its perfection'.[27] Alexei Gvozdev added that the film was 'the pride of Soviet cinema' and that even Hollywood had not managed to produce a film 'that is so captivating in its execution and at the same time so significant in its content'.[28] As with *Strike*, however, some Soviet filmmakers were less enthusiastic. Kuleshov, for example, replied to a questionnaire issued by ARK (Association of Revolutionary Cinema) by stating, 'I refrain from answering questions about the script and direction. The work of the cameraman is highly satisfactory.'[29] While Kuleshov here was damning Tisse with faint praise, his views on Eisenstein left little room for doubt, despite his notionally tight-lipped reply. Alexei Gan, it would seem, concurred with Kuleshov. His comments, though equally brief, were more severe: 'It is an eclectic work, on the strictly esthetic level. The work of the cameraman is good, but bittersweet . . . On the whole it is a bad picture.'[30] Even Vsevolod Pudovkin, describing the film as 'beautiful cinema . . . of high tension and powerful impression', could not refrain from describing the acting as 'depressingly banal'.[31]

Contemporary audience reaction has proven more difficult to gauge. Certainly the Soviet authorities claimed *Potemkin* as a popular success, citing greater box-office receipts than for Douglas Fairbanks's *Robin Hood*, running simultaneously in the same theatres.[32] However, Lunacharsky's later suggestion that *Potemkin* had difficulty attracting audiences seems to cast some doubt over these claims. Distribution difficulties, not least the limited number of prints as a consequence of a shortage of film stock, certainly did not help matters. Indeed it took several months before the movie was shown in the more distant reaches of Soviet territory. Notoriously, the citizens of Odessa, some of whom had played their part as extras in *Potemkin*, had to wait until 1927 to see the film. Whatever the truth concerning the popularity or otherwise of *Potemkin*, what does remain clear is that Eisenstein's first two films marked a watershed in early Soviet cinema.

Both *Strike* and *Potemkin* address pre-Revolutionary events, yet they do so in distinctive ways. In *Strike*, for example, it is initially unclear whether the film is intended to recount a specific historical moment, or a more generalized notion of pre-Revolutionary labour organization and its repression. This issue is particularly confused by the appearance of one of the few named individuals, Yakov Strongin, a real-life worker known to have committed suicide at a factory in St Petersburg in 1913, thus sparking an industrial dispute. Yet, in Eisenstein's film there is no attempt to present Strongin's suicide as historically accurate, not least as many of the scenes were shot in recognizable areas of Moscow rather than St Petersburg, and also allude to labour unrest in earlier periods. Further, at the end of the film, as the camera lingers over the symbolically defeated body of the proletariat, the audience is reminded of a host of pre-Revolutionary worker uprisings at Lena, Talka, Zlatoust, Yaroslavl, Tsaritsyn and Kostroma.

Potemkin, on the other hand, is much more specific in its historical source, and Eisenstein notably undertook detailed research while preparing the scenario. A greater number of individuals is named, including the leaders of the mutiny Vakulinchuk and Matyushenko, and Eisenstein went to great lengths to represent accurately both the *Prince Potemkin* itself and the Odessa surroundings.[33] This, however, did not preclude him from suggesting explicit parallels with other historical events. For example, as he himself later claimed, the massacre on the Odessa steps additionally stood for the shooting of strikers in Baku in August 1905, as well as alluding to the events of Bloody Sunday. Similarly, he argued, 'The rotten meat came to symbolize the inhuman conditions that not only soldiers and sailors, but also the exploited workers of "the great army of labour" had to endure. The scene on deck assembled typical examples of the brutality with which the Tsarist regime suppressed any attempted protest.'[34] Thus, Eisenstein deployed a specific historical narrative to reinforce wider ideas. In *Strike*, history is presented as a means to examine the processes of labour organization, a factor made evident by the Lenin quotation that opens the film: 'The strength of the working class is organization. Without organization of the masses, the proletariat is nothing. Organized it is everything. Being organized means unity of action, the unity of practical activity.' One might even argue further that, in deploying this quotation, Eisenstein was highlighting the importance of organization and collectivity in cultural, as well as industrial, production. After all, both his theatre and his cinema work depended heavily on co-operation and mass organization. In *Potemkin*, however, he deployed history in a more synecdochal manner, using the armed uprising as a part to stand for the 1905 Revolution in its entirety and, by inference, the Bolshevik Revolution of 1917.

Both *Strike* and *Potemkin* enact their key revolutionary moments early in the plot structure – in *Strike* this occurs when the workers down tools and march out of the factory, in *Potemkin* with the overthrow of the ship's officers. Both films subsequently place great emphasis on sustaining and expanding the revolutionary moment, despite the obvious threats posed by factory bosses, corrupt policemen and Tsarist troops. In the context of the mid-1920s, this emphasis on the need to sustain the Revolution against those seeking to undermine it highlighted contemporary anxieties. The Civil War might well have been over, but concerns regarding fellow-travellers and, more worryingly, enemies within were widespread. In both movies, the death of an individual – Strongin in *Strike*, Vakulinchuk in *Potemkin* – is presented as tragic. In the wake of the recent death of Lenin, the vast crowds paying homage to Vakulinchuk's corpse laid out in Odessa harbour would certainly have carried a powerful resonance. However, here the audience was shown how mourning should be transformed into purposeful political action.

Despite the presence of named individuals within *Strike* and *Potemkin*, it is essentially the masses who become the driving force of Eisenstein's historical narrative. To emphasize the essential anonymity of the worker-hero, he cast his actors strictly according

to external appearance, each character conforming to a generalized type in which both physique and physiognomy were important
signifiers of class affiliation. When possible, he used ordinary
citizens in preference to trained actors, though members of his
Proletkult troupe were also called into action. As a result, the
workers (in *Strike*) and sailors (in *Potemkin*), especially those seen
as most committed to the cause, are invariably rugged of body,
their physical being a notional product of the harsh conditions
under which they laboured in pre-Revolutionary times.
This physical strength is contrasted with the debilitated or
grotesque forms of the bourgeois enemy, thus signifying the
inevitability of the victory of the workers.

It is in the crowd scenes, however, that the mass truly attains
its heroic status. In *Strike*, for example, during the initial uprising,
the crowd of workers is represented sweeping through the factory
dragging everything – including, seemingly, Tisse's camera – in its
wake. Here Eisenstein is clearly alluding to the power of nature
as the crowd builds from a trickle into a stream, from a stream
into a river, and from a river into a torrent. In *Potemkin*, Eisenstein
repeats this flowing-water metaphor in the movement of the
masses towards the harbour after the arrival of the *Prince Potemkin*.
Starting with small tributaries, the crowd flows gradually into the
main body of the metaphorical river, passing along roadways and
under bridges on its way to the shore, where Vakulinchuk's body
is lying to be mourned. Here, the sheer force of humanity on the
move becomes a metaphor for the inexorable dynamism of
the Revolution, as unstoppable as the waves smashing against the
breakwater in the opening sequence of *Potemkin*.

Two significant shifts in plot, however, distinguish *Potemkin*
from its predecessor. Firstly, whereas *Strike* emphasizes the
massacre of workers alone, the victims of Tsarist oppression on
the Odessa steps are from a much wider class base, including shop-
keepers, students and middle-class women. As David Bordwell has

argued, this widening of victimhood serves further to alienate and demonize the former regime.[35] Here, the rallying cry 'All for one and one for all', declared in the inter-titles, serves to reinforce unconditional support for the Revolutionary cause. Secondly, where *Strike* ends in the ultimate defeat of the workers, *Potemkin* emphasizes victory, choosing, as Eisenstein argued, 'to stop the event at this point where it had become an "asset" of the revolution'.[36] Although it was widely known that the *Potemkin* mutiny ultimately failed, that the Russian navy as a whole did not overthrow its officers in 1905, and even that Matyushenko was hanged two years later, Eisenstein's positive spin seemed more in keeping with the spirit of 1926. Whether this reflected a mood of triumphalism or anxiety is a bigger question.

As has been shown, much of Eisenstein's early theatre work was characterized by its engagement with the circus aesthetic. Inevitably this carried over into both *Strike* and *Potemkin*. For example, in *Strike*, when the workers struggle to take control of the factory, Eisenstein explicitly highlights the acrobatic skills of the actors in a fight carefully choreographed into rhythmically orchestrated leaps, somersaults and clinches. To accentuate the buffoonery of the scene, one worker is laid out beneath a plank of wood only to become the fulcrum of a see-saw upon which two other workers face each other off. To add to the absurdity of the scene both combatants are sprayed with water as they see-saw back and forth, swinging first one way, then the other. Finally, as the defender of the factory is defeated, he is thrown head first into a pile of waste material where he remains, upside-down, waving his legs comically in the air. Later, when the foreman and administrator of the factory are wheeled round the yard in a barrow and dumped unceremoniously in the river, Eisenstein clearly references the slapstick of circus clowns. Such comic moments initially seem out of keeping with the seriousness of the unfolding drama. Yet Eisenstein reassures the spectator that laughter is an appropriate response by ending each sequence with a close-up of the workers themselves laughing at these circumstances. Having thus reassured the audience, however, he follows up with scenes of violence perpetrated against the workers, thus achieving a maximal shift towards disgust and anger directed against the pre-Revolutionary forces of oppression. Here such extreme shifts of mood were incorporated as part of Eisenstein's explicit strategy to shape the spectator's consciousness, directing him or her towards revolutionary fervour. In essence, Eisenstein aimed to deliver 'a series of blows to the consciousness and emotions of the audience'.[37] In contrast to the impersonal, objective cine-eye of Vertov and the *kinoki* group, he advocated using the tendentious and pugnacious cine-fist.

The most overt reference to the circus aesthetic in *Strike*, however, comes with the introduction of a group of grotesque characters, outcasts from society reduced to living in barrels on the outskirts of the city. In contrast to the strikers, these down-and-outs neither work for a living nor behave within any recognizable moral compass. Dressed in true clown style – heavily patched tailcoats, hats and galoshes – and led by their self-proclaimed 'king', this unscrupulous rabble accepts money from a police agent to loot and burn down an off-license. The striking workers are subsequently blamed for this action, thus giving the police an excuse to break up a legitimate meeting. More particularly, the barrel-dwellers perform using a variety of exaggerated gestures and acrobatics reminiscent of both circus clowns and Meyerkhold's biomechanics.

Such buffoonery is less prevalent in *Potemkin*, which adopts a more serious tone based, as Eisenstein claimed, on pathos.[38] Yet alongside the direct appeal to emotionality that constitutes one of the film's key strengths, traces of Eisenstein's fascination with the circus aesthetic can still be seen. For example, when the officers are thrown overboard, they notably perform elegant, gymnastic dives into the water. The sailors, too, clamber up the mast, climbing and swinging from ropes with all the dexterity of circus performers. As

'Mist in Odessa Harbour', *Potemkin*.

a comic touch, Eisenstein introduces the excessively hirsute priest
whose inelegant fall downstairs, reportedly performed in part by
Eisenstein himself acting as a stunt double, specifically recalls the
comic tumbles of circus clowns. In *Potemkin*, however, it is the
camera that comes to perform the most convincing gymnastics, as
Tisse ties his beloved Debrie to ropes, swinging it over the Odessa
steps to capture the effect of falling, or races it, on tracks and hand-
held, down the side of the steps to imitate the panic of those fleeing
the Tsarist troops.

Eisenstein's representation of the masses as an inexorably
flowing river was but one of many metaphors from nature
introduced into his early films. Others include the mists and setting
sun in *Potemkin*'s Odessa harbour, shrouding, literally as well as
metaphorically, Vakulinchuk's corpse. More frequently, however,
Eisenstein introduced metaphors from the animal world as a

means to direct the emotions of his audience. Thus, in *Strike*, the first halcyon days of the strike, when the workers enjoy leisure time with their families, are interspersed with shots of ducklings, piglets and kittens living a natural, carefree existence. As Eisenstein later pointed out, 'I wanted to incite in the viewer's mind an instinctive association with something plushy, pleasant, velvety and domestic because this part of my film is about the joy of waking up and not having to go to work.'[39] Similarly, he presents a bird roosting on the factory whistle on the first morning of the strike, its spontaneous song substituting for the regimented daily call to the workers. To reinforce further the idleness of the factory, a pigeon flutters among the now inactive machines, reintroducing a sense of the natural world into the unnatural, artificial space.

In a similar, if more gruesome, vein, the decaying bodies of dead cats are suspended from a scaffold in the opening sequence to the barrel-dweller scene, this time to convey negative associations. Of all the sequences in *Strike*, however, that most frequently discussed is the culminating scene in which the massacre of the workers is inter-cut with scenes from a real slaughterhouse. Here Eisenstein attempts to reinforce the sense of horror by associating the bourgeoisie's attack on the workers with the real slaughter of a bull. To intensify the emotional response, he allows the camera to linger over the gruesome scene, never flinching as the animal's throat is cut, its eyes roll, and its legs kick desperately in its death throes. The scene can only be described as truly shocking, to modern sensibilities as much as Eisenstein intended it to be for contemporary audiences.

The most explicit metaphorical reference to animals, however, comes with the introduction of the spies employed by the police to infiltrate the workers' community. These are variously identified by their animal nicknames – Fox, Bulldog, Owl and Monkey – each associated with the caricatured physiognomic and personality traits of the individual spies. Here, Eisenstein alludes to the work of

'Workers on a Scaffold', *Strike*, 1925.

the French nineteenth-century caricaturist J. J. Grandville, whose detailed drawings representing human bodies with animal heads he had seen in his childhood. Indeed, while still a small boy Eisenstein had himself produced an illustrated story recounting a day in the life of his parents in which all the characters were portrayed with the heads of various animals, including dogs, birds, frogs and even a rhinoceros.[40]

Eisenstein, however, does not confine his animal metaphors to negative characters, also drawing parallels between the workers and animals. For example, in the first part of *Strike*, the workers are shown gathered together in a host of unusual spaces. First they are perched, like a flock of birds, on a steel scaffold high above the ground. Shot from below, they are seemingly as comfortable high up in the air as they are on the ground. Forced to move on by the attention of the factory spies, they next swim skilfully, like a school of fish, among boats moored at the docks, or climb up ropes to perch on an anchor and dive gracefully from boat decks. Similarly, they clamber, like monkeys, over machines, leaping from gantries and swinging from suspended, liana-like ropes. When forced to seek out new hiding places, they uncover nest-like nooks and crannies provided by concrete tunnels and piles of rusting components, the industrial detritus of the factory. As Yuri Tsivian has indicated, the confidence, grace and agility with which the workers move around the factory spaces – their notional 'urban jungle' – contrasts dramatically with the clumsiness of the bourgeoisie. Yet it is also worth noting that Eisenstein is here making a 'pack' analogy, the workers' collectivity notably distinguished from the 'individual' animals associated with the police spies.

One of the main functions of these animal metaphors is to reinforce an allusion to the tense relationship between the bosses and workers as that of the hunter and the hunted. Yet, the question of who is the hunter and who the hunted never remains stable. In one scene the spies pursue the workers, in another the workers pursue the spies. To reinforce the hunt metaphor, fences, cages and other barriers make regular appearances throughout *Strike*. Whether it is the animals in cages in the pet shop scene near the start of the film, or the prisoners in the police cell towards the conclusion, incarceration is a recurring theme, while walls, gateways and fences consistently act as metaphors for the division between the workers and their oppressors. Notably, it is the storming of these barriers, whether it be the workers storming the factory gates or the soldiers breaking into the workers' quarters, that drives Eisenstein's narrative along. Ultimately, the final capture and massacre of the workers, herded together under powerful water jets, only serves to reinforce the centrality of the hunting theme, the all too vivid, blood-lust slaughter of the bull further confirming that it is 'the kill' that brings about the ultimate resolution of the plot.

Animal metaphors might, at first glance, seem less prevalent in *Potemkin*. Yet, handled with greater subtlety, they lie just beneath

'Sailors in Hammocks', *Potemkin*, 1926.

the surface. For example, an early scene focuses on the sailors
asleep in their hammocks, suspended from ropes in the bowels of
the ship. As the camera moves closely among the throng of men,
destabilizing the viewer's sense of perspective, the shrouded figures
begin to resemble prey, bound and trapped in a vast spider's web.
The sole guard, strolling freely among the confusion of ropes and
bodies, beats one sailor randomly, suggesting once more his role as
dominant hunter. Alternatively these hammocks might be read as
cocoons, enclosing creatures yet to emerge into the light of day.
This potential metaphor is reinforced towards the end of the scene,
when Vakulinchuk declares that now is the time to rise up and join
all of Russia in its struggle against the forces of oppression. One by
one the men emerge sleepily from their cocoons, transforming
themselves from an inert group of individuals into a potentially
dynamic collective force.

The insect metaphor is further developed in the scene in which the sailors refuse the maggot-ridden meat. Here, the medical officer, Dr Smirnov, who declares the meat fit to eat, is excessively diminutive in size and stature, described by Eisenstein as 'short', 'weedy' and with 'shifty eyes'.[41] Equating the ruling classes with parasites feeding off the flesh of the proletariat was a familiar-enough trope in the mid-1920s, and here the officious, punctilious and sour Dr Smirnov fulfils his role admirably. Further, Eisenstein reinforces this metaphor in the scene in which Dr Smirnov is cast into the water by the sailors. Now the camera cuts back to a close-up of the maggots while the sailors declare that Smirnov has 'gone to feed the fishes'.

Perhaps the most striking animal metaphor in *Potemkin*, however, comes in the famous stone-lion sequence. In retaliation for the Odessa-steps massacre, the *Prince Potemkin* aims its guns towards the town and fires on the General Headquarters. As walls tumble and smoke billows, the camera zooms in on three consecutive shots of marble lions (notably filmed in the Alupka Palace, some 300 kilometres from Odessa harbour), the first recumbent, the second raising its head, and the third on its haunches. Yet, despite constituting one of the most dramatic examples of an Eisensteinian 'attraction' – a visual counterpoint, as he himself declared, to the verbal statement 'and the stones roared' – it remains unclear who the lions are supposed to represent.[42] Is it the Tsarist generals, angered by the bombardment, or the Russian people raised into action by the Odessa-steps outrage? Does the scene signify revolution or reaction?

Much has also been made of Eisenstein's use of geometrical forms in his early movies. Thus, David Bordwell has highlighted the extensive use of the circle as a recurring motif in *Strike*.[43] Initially appearing as the letter 'o' in an inter-title (part of the Russian word 'not', or 'but') and thence transformed, through a dissolve edit, into a spinning factory wheel, the circle motif serves to symbolize the unity of the workers and the productivity of the machine. Eisenstein further emphasizes the circular form by focusing on close-ups of eyes and optical equipment, thus signifying

'The Alupka Lions', *Potemkin*.

notions of vision and surveillance. Intriguingly, *Potemkin* redeploys the circle motif, again using close-ups of eyes in constant scrutiny or focusing on searchlights operating as mechanical eyes. The circle also appears in the form of the port-hole, through which both food and arms are supplied to the sailors; the plate, upon which the ironic words 'Give us this Day our Daily Bread' appear to one frustrated sailor; and the barrels of the big guns, pointed directly towards the audience.

Perhaps the triangle marks a more forceful recurring motif in *Potemkin*. This aggressively dynamic form, epitomized in El Lissitzky's famous poster *Beat the Whites with the Red Wedge* (1919), appears in several guises throughout the film. The previously mentioned hammocks, for example, form an intricate criss-crossing of triangular shapes, while the sails of both schooners and skiffs in Odessa harbour repeat this form. Similarly, the dead Vakulinchuk is laid to rest in a triangular tent, shot from both outside and inside to emphasize its geometry. Throughout the movie triangles are emphasized through shots composed with either the mass crowds, the Odessa steps themselves, or the ship's guns dissecting the screen from corner to corner. The most dynamic deployment of the form, however, comes in the final shot as the gigantic prow of the *Prince Potemkin*, its deck lined with sailors cheering triumphantly, moves inexorably towards the screen, its massive form overwhelming the spectator and seemingly threatening to destroy the entire auditorium. In an ironic echo of the opening scenes of waves crashing against a breakwater, it is now the mutinous sailors who unleash a force greater than nature itself, the unstoppable force of revolution. Eisenstein's ambitious and unrealized original idea for the premiere of *Potemkin*, to have the cinema screen ripped apart at this point to reveal the actual sailors on stage, further suggests the vitality and dramatic force of this moment.

Eisenstein's extraordinary breadth of cultural knowledge certainly informed his filmmaking at every stage of production,

'Triangular Forms', *Potemkin*.

from the framing of the individual shot to the fully edited montage sequence. Further, he was always willing to embrace any style, technique or device that served his particular purpose. Paraphrasing Voltaire, he later claimed that 'Art admits all efforts except those that fail to achieve their end.'[44] In cinematic terms, for example, his early movies owe a significant debt to the work of D. W. Griffith, not least his 1916 epic production *Intolerance*.[45] Later, Eisenstein would acknowledge that Griffith was nothing short of a 'revelation' for young Soviet filmmakers in the early 1920s.[46] In thematic terms, for example, the foregrounding of persecution, exploitation and social injustice in Eisenstein's first two movies inevitably recalls one of the four interwoven episodes in *Intolerance*, in which labour unrest, false accusation and a strike all take centre stage. In one scene, troops are called in to break the strike and march, mechanistically, towards randomly fleeing strikers, firing indiscriminately. Though Griffith's editing hardly carries the same intensity and impact of Eisenstein's later Odessa-steps sequence, the similarities are at least worthy of mention.

It was more in stylistic and technical terms, however, that Griffith's work was to leave its mark on Eisenstein. In particular, Griffith pioneered non-linear time editing and the fast interspersing of close-up and distant shots, montage techniques introduced to enhance both the narrative and the aesthetic possibilities of the cinematic medium, adding mood, sensitivity and emotion to his storytelling. Perhaps most significantly, *Intolerance*, like Griffith's earlier epic *Birth of a Nation* (1915), concludes with a high-tempo pursuit using both rhythmic and accelerated editing – each sequence becoming shorter and shorter in length – to build to a crescendo of energy and dynamism. All of these techniques would play a major part in Eisenstein's first two productions.

Griffith was not the only director to influence Eisenstein. For example, when one of the police spies in *Strike* disguises himself as a blind beggar, Eisenstein uses a dissolve, removing the false beard and glasses and thus 'uncovering' the spy. Though something of a cinematic cliché by 1925, this device had earlier become synonymous with Louis Feuillade's *Fantômas* movies of 1913–14, which Eisenstein had enjoyed as a child.[47] Similarly, when Eisenstein portrays the interior of the factory owner's mansion, his emphasis on the neo-Classical grandeur of the space, with its ponderous, empty rooms and excess of columns, is virtually a direct quotation from the melodramas of the pre-Revolutionary Russian filmmaker Yevgeny Bauer. That Bauer's films, including *Song of Triumphant Love* (1915) and *A Life for a Life* (1916), so popular before the Revolution, were now out of favour only served to reinforce the socio-political significance of Eisenstein's visual reference.[48] From the slapstick of *Strike* to a 'western'-style gunfight during the mutiny sequence in *Potemkin*, his first two movies are full of quotations from the early history of cinematography.

Nor was it just cinematic works that influenced Eisenstein. Indeed, much of the visual impact of his early films derives from the sheer richness and diversity of early Soviet visual culture. Political posters, Constructivist experimental works, even the realist paintings of the cultural right, all provided contemporary models. For example, as Roberta Reeder has pointed out, in *Strike*, Eisenstein's extensive use of caricature to parody the bourgeoisie is heavily reminiscent of early Soviet political posters, especially those produced by Mayakovsky for the Russian Telegraph Agency, known under the acronym ROSTA. Drawing on the conventions of pre-Revolutionary satire, ROSTA artists invariably personified capitalism as a corpulent, cigar-smoking, top-hatted businessman, just as Eisenstein would in the opening sequences of his first film. Similarly, ROSTA posters frequently represented the worker in stark silhouette, a consequence of crude production techniques and a means by which to emphasize the anonymity of the worker-hero. Eisenstein, too, would frequently shoot his workers and sailors against the light, emphasizing their sharp, non-individualized outlines. By linking his visual vocabulary with that of early political posters, he familiarized his audiences with both the subject of his films and their agitational intentions.

Other influential sources can be identified in *Strike* and *Potemkin*. The visual vocabulary of Russian Constructivism is evoked in their emphasis on industrial machinery and the framing of individual shots to highlight sharp geometrical, quasi-abstract forms. Further, it could be argued that Eisenstein's cinematic technique itself sought to expose, rather than disguise, the production processes of filmmaking, thus making visible the structural principles of his art. In this way, both *Strike* and *Potemkin* can be interpreted as engaging with the central ideological tenets of Russian Constructivism. Further, Eisenstein's emphasis on the mass rather than the individual can be read as a form of re-enacting on celluloid the plethora of theatrical pageants and parades that dominated the early Soviet period.

Eisenstein's first two films also drew upon widely divergent contemporary practices in painting and sculpture. The early 1920s witnessed something of a revival of figurative art, not least as a backlash against the extreme views of the more iconoclastic members of the avant-garde, including Nikolai Tarabukin's 1923 pronouncement of the 'death of painting'.[49] Into this highly volatile climate, a whole host of new art groups emerged, each arguing for its own hegemony and resisting the claims of rival groups. On the far right of the spectrum lay AKhRR (Association of Artists of Revolutionary Russia), a realist-inspired group whose declared ambition was 'to set down, artistically and documentarily, the revolutionary impulse of this great moment of history'.[50] AKhRR's emphasis on documentary chimed sympathetically with the views of Vertov's *kinoki* group, though neither side would comfortably have seen themselves as allies. Similarly, AKhRR's passion for representing Revolutionary history would closely parallel the dominant historical themes within Eisenstein's early cinematic productions. Once again, however, any

'Three Workers', *Strike*, 1925.

claims of allegiance would have been strongly resisted, not least as Eisenstein's affiliation with the LEF group would have been viewed as anathema to AKhRR. Yet it is at least noteworthy that, despite such stark ideological differences, there are a number of overlaps between these two seemingly opposed cultural models. For example, the factory landscapes in *Strike* and the numerous portraits of heroic workers and sailors in both it and *Potemkin*, taken in isolation, can be read as virtual blueprints for AKhRR-style painting. Similarly, AKhRR works, such as Nikolai Kasatkin's *Miners Changing Shift* (1923) and Georgy Savitsky's *Red Leather-Tanning Factory* (1924), the latter notably set in an abattoir, could be mistaken for stills from *Strike*. To take a more specific example, Eisenstein concludes the second reel of that film with a carefully framed shot of three workers of varying age (similar worker-portraits appear in *Potemkin*). This group portrait of archetypal proletarian identity inevitably recalls portraits by Fyodor Bogorodsky, Viktor Perelman and Yevgeny Katsman, leading exponents of AKhRR. Eisenstein's new triumvirate of workers, however, might also be read as a striking modernization of the most famous artwork in Russia, Andrei Rublev's fifteenth-century *Trinity* icon, at that time on display at the Tretyakov Gallery in Moscow.

Yet a closer parallel to Eisenstein's position might be found in those artists associated with the more experimental wing of figuration. Many of these painters, including Alexander Deineka and Yuri Pimenov from OST (the Society of Easel Painters), were striving to find a middle ground between the avant-gardism of the Constructivists and the realism of AKhRR. Works such as Deineka's series of illustrations of miners in the Donbass, published in 1924 in the journal *At the Bench*, attempted to forge a new Heroic Realism that celebrated labour through the representation of the anonymous worker, but did not reject expressive and dynamic formal techniques. OST's ideas seemed to run parallel to those of Eisenstein, and there is certainly an affinity between their works and his early films. However, this relationship was far from being a one-way thing. Indeed, the industrial subjects of Deineka and Pimenov, such as *Building New Factories* (1926) and *You Give Heavy Industry* (1927), seem to owe more than a passing debt to the visual impact of Eisenstein's films. Deineka, in particular, in works such as *The Defence of Petrograd* (1927), drew heavily on Eisenstein's frequent use of dramatic crossing walkways and balconies, features that appear in both *Strike* and *Potemkin*.

What matters here is less a sense of primacy, of who was influenced by whom, and more the fact that these parallels reveal the sheer diversity of visual vocabularies available to artists during the decade after the October Revolution. That Eisenstein so readily embraced this vast range of material reflects the astonishing eclecticism of his own sensibilities as well as that of the cultural-historical moment in which his early movies were produced.

In an unpublished article written shortly after *Potemkin* was completed, Eisenstein directly compared his first two films. *Potemkin*, he claimed, was 'not a continuation of *Strike*, but a contrast to it'.[51] This, he continued, did not reflect a radical change in approach, but rather an acknowledgement of the changing nature of the audience and the need to adopt new strategies to ensure maximum impact. Here, in effect, he was attempting to justify what many perceived to be the more traditional aspects of *Potemkin*, not least its deployment of pathos and its strong appeal to the emotions. In drawing a parallel with the economic 'step backwards' instigated by the NEP, Eisenstein was arguing that the reintroduction of such devices as 'doubt, tears, sentiment, lyricism, psychologism, maternal feelings, etc' was effectively a form of cultural NEP, a necessary turning backwards to more traditional cultural methods as a means to direct, most effectively, the political education of the audience.[52] 'The current phase of audience reaction', he continued, 'determines our methods of influence: what it reacts to. Without this *there can be no influential art and certainly no art with maximum influenc*e.'[53] His more emphatic claim that '*Strike* is a treatise, *Potemkin* is a hymn' reinforced in more poetic terms this notional deployment of different strategies to attain the same ends.[54] Yet, it also tells us a great deal about the difficult context in which he was working. The enormous cultural divisions of the mid-1920s, pitching traditionalists against modernists, documentary makers against dramatists, artists against engineers, all served to make any cultural intervention fraught with controversy and, occasionally, contradiction. In the end, the greatest strength of Eisenstein's early cinematic work, as articulated in his first two productions, lies less in the innovations so often celebrated than in an extraordinary ability to synthesize coherently such disparate ideas and influences.

3

Transition

'At twenty-seven the boy from Riga became a celebrity.'[1]

In March 1926 Eisenstein and his cameraman Tisse travelled to Berlin to attend the international premiere of *Potemkin*. On a more personal note, the trip gave Eisenstein an opportunity to visit his father's grave for the first time. During their five-week sojourn, he and Tisse sought out members of the German film industry. At the UFA studios they were introduced to Fritz Lang and his screenwriter wife Thea von Harbou, at that time working on their blockbuster production *Metropolis*, and met the influential German cameramen Karl Freund and Günther Rittau. Later, they visited the set of another new UFA production, *Faust*, directed by F. W. Murnau and starring the well-known actor Emil Jannings. Neither Lang nor Murnau had much time for Eisenstein, whose international reputation was still far from established. The release of *Potemkin* in Germany would soon change all that. But first there were a number of obstacles to overcome.

Shortly after Eisenstein's arrival in Berlin, a report was submitted to the Reich Commissar for Supervision of Public Order demanding that *Potemkin* be banned on the grounds that it potentially inspired revolutionary activity. Given Eisenstein's earlier argument that 'there should be no cinema other than agit-cinema' and that the Soviet state valued *Potemkin* specifically for its agitational qualities, it is, perhaps, difficult to argue with the logic here.[2]

Despite opposition, however, *Potemkin*'s German distributors secured a public licence permitting it to be released. An unfortunate consequence of the delay, however, was that the premiere was held up until 29 April 1926, three days after Eisenstein and Tisse had returned to Moscow.[3]

The debate generated by the German release of *Potemkin* sparked a major controversy. The German army, for example, expressly forbade all personnel from attending the film, even going so far as to place plain-clothes guards at the entrances to some cinemas.[4] In a similarly anxious vein, the final scenes from *Potemkin* led to questions being asked in the Reichstag concerning the military threat posed by the Soviet fleet. Ironically, Eisenstein had actually used newsreel footage of the American navy for these scenes.[5] In May, the controversy was further stepped up when Douglas Fairbanks and Mary Pickford arrived in Berlin as part of a European tour and expressed an interest in viewing *Potemkin*. An exclusive screening was soon organized for the Hollywood stars, accompanied by an entire orchestra playing Edmund Meisel's newly commissioned score. Immediately afterwards, Fairbanks declared that viewing *Potemkin* had been 'the most intense and profoundest experience of [his] life'.[6] Press reports of this comment soon ensured that Eisenstein's movie attracted worldwide attention.

The following month, calls were renewed for the banning of *Potemkin*, described by one German politician as 'an insidious and dangerous beast, which has seized the State by the throat'.[7] Yet this only served to fan the flames and led to the staunch defence of the film by left-wing libertarians, many of whom were far more concerned with resisting censorship than supporting *Potemkin*. Thus, by the summer of 1926 right and left in German politics could largely be defined by attitudes towards Eisenstein's film. In the end, the controversy served to ensure that it remained a cause célèbre, the must-see movie of the age. Despite persistent political intervention, the film was widely distributed throughout the nation, attracting large audiences, many notably in excess of its release back home. Shortly afterwards, *Potemkin* was exported to other countries and generated a similar stir. In Britain, in the wake of the General Strike, Stanley Baldwin's Conservative administration considered it far too revolutionary and banned its public release. Mischievously, the Soviet press took great glee in reporting that the authoritarian Home Secretary Sir William Joynson-Hicks had signed the prohibition order without even having seen the film.[8] Italy, Spain, Denmark, Norway and the Baltic republics soon followed suit. In France, too, *Potemkin* was denied commercial release, though there the efforts of Léon Moussinac, the French Communist and Soviet cinema enthusiast, ensured that *Potemkin*, along with other Soviet films, was privately screened in his club, 'Les Amis de Spartacus'.

The situation in the United States was less clear cut. Although the worst excesses of the so-called 'Red Scare' were now in the past, anxieties regarding Bolshevism abounded, and protests were inevitably raised regarding the film's release. In Pennsylvania, for example, it was banned outright. However, in December 1926 the film was officially premiered at the Biltmore Theatre in New York. John Grierson, subsequently to become Britain's most celebrated early documentary filmmaker, edited the film for American audiences. There can be little doubt that the support of Hollywood luminaries, including Fairbanks and Pickford, did much to secure this release. Charlie Chaplin was also to lend his support, declaring *Potemkin* 'the best film in the world'.[9]

The critical success of *Potemkin* in the international arena caught the Soviet authorities somewhat by surprise. Doubtless they valued the fact that the publicity surrounding the film raised the profile and, not insignificantly, the profit margin for many later Soviet films. However, and perhaps more worryingly, all the evidence suggested that this success was heavily dependent upon the support not of the working masses, but of an elite intelligentsia far more interested in the aesthetics of cinema than the politics of Bolshevism. While the film doubtless gained sympathy for the Soviet Union, it was hardly, as some of its staunchest opponents feared, a catalyst for World Revolution. In a telling phrase, Cal York, the critic for *Photoplay Magazine*, observed, 'After witnessing it, nobody went Bolshevik, but a lot of people left with some pretty revolutionary ideas about film making.'[10]

For Eisenstein, the success of *Potemkin* was a life-transforming experience. Virtually overnight he became an international celebrity courted by the rich and famous. Up until the mid-1920s, the possibilities for travel between the Soviet Union and the wider international community had been largely limited, not least as many Western states refused to recognize the legitimacy of the Soviet government. In 1925, however, things began to change. In an attempt to develop closer international ties and enhance its reputation abroad, the Soviet authorities established VOKS (Society for Cultural Relations with Foreign Countries). Attracting tourists and, more pragmatically, hard currency was a key objective here. Initial success was sporadic, and it was not until the establishment of Intourist in 1929 that visitor numbers began to grow substantially. Nonetheless, among the relatively few Western visitors to Moscow in 1926 and '27, many were notably beating a path directly to the door of a small flat in Chistye Prudy, the home of Sergei Eisenstein.

In July 1926, for example, Fairbanks and Pickford arrived in Moscow, where they were mobbed by adoring fans. The presence of Hollywood's golden couple generated a veritable press frenzy and even led to the somewhat opportunist production of a movie entitled *The Kiss of Mary Pickford*, in which newsreel footage of the visit was surreptitiously integrated into a comic plot critiquing the excesses of fame.[11] When Fairbanks and Pickford were introduced to Eisenstein, they were given a print of *Potemkin* to take back to the United States. In return they invited Eisenstein to Hollywood to make a movie for United Artists, thus considerably enhancing the Soviet director's reputation both at home and abroad. As Eisenstein later recalled gleefully, 'Doug and Mary travelled to Moscow to shake the hand of the boy from Riga – he had made *Potemkin*.'[12]

Soon other figures from the world of culture arrived at Eisenstein's door. From the United States came the writers Theodore Dreiser, Sinclair Lewis and John Dos Passos, the academic Henry Dana, and the journalists Louis Fischer and Joseph Freeman. Alfred H. Barr, future director of the Museum of Modern Art in New York, was introduced to Eisenstein in December 1927. Among the Europeans were Moussinac from France, the artist Käthe Kollwitz and the dancer Valeska Gert, both from Germany, and the Swiss architect Le Corbusier. When the Mexican muralist Diego Rivera spent the best part of a year in Moscow working for the Soviet government, he too was introduced to Eisenstein. Four years later, Rivera would be the first to welcome Eisenstein to Mexico during his ill-fated expedition to make *Qué Viva México!*

Brimming with confidence, Eisenstein now began to plan his next production, a proposed collaboration with Sergei Tretyakov based on the writer's successful stage production, *Roar China!* (1926).[13] Tretyakov's forceful critique of Western imperialism and class exploitation certainly suggested itself as an ideal vehicle for another revolutionary film. Thus, in an optimistic vein, he and Eisenstein applied for funds to travel to China to make the movie in situ. Their request, however, was turned down. While it is impossible to determine precisely why this was, several factors may have played a part. Firstly, despite the profits from *Potemkin*, hard currency was still in relatively short supply, thus restricting opportunities for international travel. Secondly, the political situation in China had recently taken a turn for the worse, with Chiang Kai-shek's Nationalist revolutionaries splitting from the recently formed Chinese Communist Party. A more compelling reason to reject Eisenstein's application, however, may well have been an official desire to secure the young director's talents for more domestic projects. Since December 1924, Stalin's call for 'socialism in one country', delivered as a notable rebuff to Trotsky's demand for 'permanent revolution', was gaining increasing support and authority. As World Revolution no longer looked a likely proposition, the consolidation of the Soviet state, both politically and economically, was increasingly a top priority. Here, Soviet cinema had a key role to play.

In 1926, Eisenstein was commissioned by Sovkino to work on two major film projects, *October* and *The General Line*, later retitled *The Old and the New*. Both were domestic in focus, the former celebrating the victory of the Bolshevik Party in bringing about revolution, the latter the continuing struggle to bring revolutionary values to the countryside. Doubtless, Sovkino expected Eisenstein to replicate the cinematic style that had brought *Potemkin* such success. What they had not counted on was his restless experimentalism. Drawing on some of the more radical discoveries of *Potemkin*, Eisenstein now sought to develop a new kind of cinematic language, one he would later designate 'intellectual' cinema. In the end, both *October* and *The General Line* marked a major transition in Eisenstein's filmmaking. However, the films failed to appeal to the critics who had previously supported him and ultimately led to a significant decline in his reputation.

Although not finally released until a year and a half after *October*, Eisenstein's first official commission of 1926 was for *The General Line*. While *Potemkin* was whipping up a storm in Europe, Eisenstein and Alexandrov were back in Moscow preparing the scenario for this new commission. In July they began shooting scenes in villages around Moscow. *The General Line* was intended to reflect political policy as established at the Fourteenth Party Congress of 1925. Having ostensibly secured the cities, the Soviet authorities remained painfully aware of a lack of support in rural regions. As 80 per cent of the population lived in the countryside, gaining the support of the peasantry was seen as crucial to the continued success of the Revolution. Yet this would be no easy task. During the Civil War, the Red Army expropriations of grain and other food supplies had done little to endear the Bolsheviks to the rural masses, not least as these actions were widely held to have led to the widespread famines of 1921–2, resulting in millions of deaths. Further, Bolshevik attitudes towards the peasantry often left a lot to be desired. As the urban proletariat was regarded as the vanguard of Revolutionary consciousness, so the peasantry was held to be little more than an uneducated rabble, inclined to cling to age-old traditions and resist modernization. Herein lay a dilemma. On the one hand, the survival of the state depended entirely on the countryside producing enough food to feed the cities, and thus the peasantry needed to be kept on side. However, the Soviet authorities also wanted to encourage the deployment of modern farming methods and suspected that coercion might be required to implement such changes. In 1926, official policy declared that the modernization of the countryside was necessary, but accepted that this would inevitably be slow. In particular, it was agreed that the free market economy of NEP was essential to ensure stability in the countryside. Modernization therefore was presented as a distant aspiration more than an immediate command.

The General Line thus set out to offer an inspirational example of the potential for change, a vision for the future rather than a reflection of the present. In essence it told the story of a peasant woman whose individual efforts succeeded in introducing collectivization to a remote rural commune. Here, the casting of the central character was crucial, and Eisenstein once more rejected professional actors, seeking a genuine peasant woman to play the part. Eventually, he settled on the exquisitely characterful Marfa Lapkina, whose hardened, determined yet optimistic features added enormously to the appeal of the movie. Although the initial plan was to name this character Yevdokiya Ukraintseva, specifically to symbolize the importance of Ukraine as an agricultural region, Lapkina retained her real name in the final version of the film.[14] Further, Eisenstein insisted that she return to her village after filming was completed. Once more, he was careful to combine the documentary and the dramatic, thus blurring the line between reality and fiction. Filming continued throughout the summer of 1926, as Eisenstein and his crew moved from village to village, but progress was severely hampered by poor weather. The crew was eventually forced to head south to seek better light and continued shooting until late in the year.

In the end, however, it was not the weather that stalled progress on *The General Line*. In September 1926, plans were already underway to stage a series of major cultural events to celebrate the tenth anniversary of the October Revolution. Several film dramas recounting the events of 1917 had already been commissioned,

'Lenin's Arrival at the Finland Station', *October*, 1928.

Sergei Eisenstein
demonstrating
Lenin's gesture
during the filming
of *October*.

including Vsevolod Pudovkin's *The End of St Petersburg* and Boris
Barnet's *Moscow in October*. Dziga Vertov and Esfir Shub had also
begun work on major documentaries.[15] Aware of Eisenstein's newly
established reputation as the pre-eminent figure in Soviet cinematography, the Anniversary Committee called on the director of
Potemkin to work on what would be billed as the most important of
these productions: a history of the Revolution to be titled *October*.
This was an offer that Eisenstein could not, and would not, refuse.

Given the importance of the commission, official interference
was inevitable. First, Eisenstein was advised to consult the American
writer John Reed's famous first-hand account of the Revolution,
Ten Days That Shook the World (1919). Second, despite Eisenstein's
previous emphasis on the masses rather than the individual, he

was put under pressure to include Lenin in his narrative. He once more refused to use a professional actor, however, and launched a search for someone who resembled the dead Soviet leader, eventually settling on an unknown worker by the name of Vasily Nikandrov. Yet, even this decision opened Eisenstein to much criticism among the cultural fraternity. For example, both Osip Brik and Esfir Shub decried the decision to use an actor to represent Lenin, while Mayakovsky went so far as to declare that he would hurl eggs at any fake Lenin appearing on screen.[16] Thankfully, the poet failed to live up to his rhetorical promise.

Working closely with Alexandrov, Eisenstein completed the first script for *October* in early 1927 and sent it to the Anniversary Committee for approval. Initially, he had proposed a sweeping panorama, covering the build-up to the Revolution and continuing into the Civil War era. In its final manifestation, however, *October* covered the period from the February Revolution of 1917 to the storming of the Winter Palace on the night of 7/8 November. In March, the crew set out for Leningrad; within a few weeks, shooting was in full swing. During the summer months Eisenstein virtually took control of the city. The Red Army, fire crews and city officials were all placed at his disposal, and, when power was needed to light Palace Square, the supply to the rest of the city was switched off. Eisenstein was also given complete access to the Winter Palace and the Smolny, the Revolution's two main historical sites. Shooting continued throughout the summer and autumn before Eisenstein returned to Moscow to complete the opening sequence, re-enacting the demolition of the monument to Tsar Alexander III. By now, however, pressure was mounting, and, with filming still taking place as late as mid-October 1927, the likelihood of completing the final editing in time for the proposed anniversary screening began to look increasingly unlikely. By the beginning of November, after weeks of working every waking hour, the strain began to show, and Eisenstein fell ill. On medical advice, he was confined to his bed. Thus, on the anniversary of the Revolution, the Bolshoi Theatre played host to only two of the three proposed historical dramatizations, Pudovkin and Barnet having completed their commissions. Only selected scenes from Eisenstein's unfinished *October* were shown.

Once recovered, Eisenstein returned to work, completing a first version in mid-January 1928. By now he had edited out most of the scenes featuring Trotsky, reputedly at Stalin's personal command, following the expulsion of the former head of the Red Army. *October* was rescheduled for general release on 14 March 1928, the eve of an officially constituted Party Conference on Cinema. A week before this date, Eisenstein was still arguing that more time would be necessary for the satisfactory completion of the movie.[17]

In late 1927, Eisenstein himself described *October* as 'a complete departure from the factual and the anecdotal', thus suggesting that he was seeking to move beyond the by now entrenched debate between documentary and drama.[18] *October*, he argued, 'present[ed] a new form of cinema: a collection of essays on a series of themes which constitute October'.[19] Here, Eisenstein was particularly referring to the expanded use of symbolism and metaphor which he regarded as a move towards the development of a specific cinematic language. The turning point for this aspect of his burgeoning film theory, he further claimed, was the Alupka lions sequence from *Potemkin*, which represented 'a [leap] from representation of ordinary life to abstract and generalized imagery'. For Eisenstein, *October* 'harnessed' the lions.[20] It might be argued, of course, that this deployment of symbolic and metaphorical devices was hardly a departure; indeed, much of his earlier theatre and cinema work had made use of such strategies. What distinguished *October* from his earlier work was the sheer abundance of symbols and metaphors deployed.

This new emphasis was established from the very opening shots. As the titles fade, the camera zooms in on the famous monument

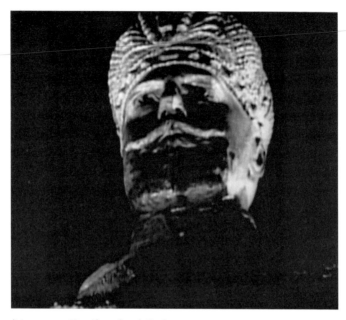

'Monument to Tsar Alexander III', *October*.

to Tsar Alexander III, the work of the sculptor Alexander
Opekushin originally erected outside the Cathedral of Christ the
Saviour in Moscow in 1912. Close-ups of the Tsar's crowned head
and the orb and sceptre held in his hands emphasize the symbols
of monarchical authority, while the inscription on the plinth iden-
tifies the figure as 'Emperor of All Russia'. Next, a peasant woman
clambers up onto the plinth and calls on the workers to join her.
They tie ropes around the head and torso of the monument and
eventually pull it to the ground. The inter-title 'February 1917'
informs the spectator that this iconoclastic act stands metaphorically for the collapse of the monarchy following the February
Revolution.

This dramatic opening sequence raises important questions
from the outset. For example, why did Eisenstein choose to focus

on Alexander III rather than Nikolai II, the actual last Tsar, to signify the oppressive authority of monarchism? Alexander III did have a reputation as one of the Russian Empire's most ruthless and authoritarian rulers. Further, the fact that Lenin's brother, Alexander Ulyanov, had been executed in 1887 for attempting to assassinate Alexander III added a political potency to the choice. Yet for Eisenstein, it was the domineering presence and ponderous, static qualities of the monument itself that served emphatically to signify the notional stability and permanence of Tsarist authority. That this archetypal immovable object – Tsarism – was so easily swept aside by the irrepressible force of Bolshevism both drama- tized and strengthened the Marxist notion of the inevitability of the Revolution.

A second question concerns the extent to which this sequence could be read in a documentary sense, as simply a historical re- enactment of an actual event. It is certainly the case that Opekushin's monument was dismantled by Bolshevik supporters, yet this took place in Moscow, not in Petrograd, and occurred not in February 1917 but after the October Revolution as part of Lenin's 1918 Plan for Monumental Propaganda. Eisenstein did use documentary evidence to inform his re-enactment, most notably a series of photographs, some of which were published in *Novy Lef* in March 1927. Esfir Shub also showed Eisenstein footage from her document- aries of 1927, including images of the fallen fragments of the monu- ment. Given this context, it is highly likely that these documentary sources stimulated the original idea.

To film the sequence, Eisenstein commissioned a full-scale plaster replica to be made and, for further authenticity, erected this against the backdrop of the Cathedral of Christ the Saviour. Yet, it should be added that Eisenstein's sequence notably departs from the photographic evidence for dramatic effect. For example, the photographs reveal that originally, scaffolding had been erect- ed around the monument, yet Eisenstein excluded this, presumably on the grounds that it would have suggested greater planning and premeditation in relation to the dismantling process.[21] Thus, in the end, Eisenstein used the photographic evidence to lend an authenticity to his dramatization, yet adapted this evidence to add a sense of energy and spontaneity to what was in fact a slow and carefully conceived process. Adopting a Marxist dialectical approach, he claimed that bringing documentary and drama together resulted in a new cinematic form, one he later described as cinema 'Beyond the Played and the Non-Played'.[22]

After this opening sequence, *October* focuses attention on the new Provisional Government under the leadership of Alexander Kerensky, highlighting its continuing ties to both Church and bourgeois society. As the first decision of the new authority is to maintain its military support for its allies in the First World War, the ideals of both workers and soldiers are already seen to be betrayed. Here, once more, Eisenstein uses montage techniques combined with metaphor to signify this betrayal. As the camera zooms in on Russian soldiers gazing fearfully upwards from a trench, close-ups of heavy artillery in a factory are rapidly interspersed. As this military hardware is lowered, seemingly directly onto the heads of the soldiers, Eisenstein invites a metaphorical reading of the state apparatus literally crushing, or oppressing, the ordinary soldier.

Next, *October* progresses to the arrival of Lenin in Petrograd. As the population rallies round the Revolutionary leader, his dynamism both literally and metaphorically whips up a storm. His revolutionary energy is thus contrasted with the torpor and indolence of Kerensky and his retinue, ensconced in the Tsar's former seat of power, the Winter Palace.

From here, the film turns its attention to the so-called 'July Days', when an abortive workers' insurrection was crushed by troops loyal to the Provisional Government. Here, the carcass of a white horse suspended from a bridge, opened to cut off the workers' district from the city, symbolizes this, albeit temporary, defeat of the forces of radicalism. Yet, at this point Eisenstein also introduces a somewhat incongruous allusion to Christian legend. A young Bolshevik agitator is attacked by a group of bourgeois ladies armed with little more than the sharp points of their umbrellas. As the young Bolshevik is literally speared to death by these otherwise innocuous symbols of bourgeois feminine identity, his martyrdom turns him into a modern-day St Sebastian.

It was Eisenstein's access to the Winter Palace, however, that enabled him to take symbolic and metaphorical montage into a whole new terrain. For example, to parody Kerensky's hunger for power and self-elevation, Eisenstein shows him repeatedly ascending the Jordan staircase while cuts to inter-titles list new, ever more grandiose, titles acquired along the way. When Kerensky approaches the summit and stands before the chamber of the former Tsarina, whose first name and patronymic, Alexandra Fyodorevna, echo in feminized versions his own, he pauses beneath an allegorical statue holding aloft a wreath. The low angle of the shot is calculated to give the impression that Kerensky is now being crowned, thus reinforcing the spectre that the Provisional Government is simply a new version of the same old monarchy.

It was not just the physical spaces of the Winter Palace, how-ever, that provided ample opportunity for such cinematic strategies. Among Eisenstein's most controversial sequences were those that focused on the numerous decorative objects and artefacts found within the former Tsarist residence. To take one of the better-known examples, Kerensky's entrance into the Tsarina's chamber is juxtaposed with a close-up of a mechanical peacock turning its rear to the spectator and, seemingly, Kerensky. On one level, the use of montage to juxtapose the leader of the Provisional Government with a mechanical toy serves to diminish the authority and importance of Kerensky, presenting him as little more than a plaything of the former regime. Moreover, the linking

'The Mechanical Peacock', *October*.

of Kerensky specifically with this bird furthers the notion of his self-absorbed and preening nature; Kerensky, here, is as vain as a peacock. Later film critics have taken the interpretation of this scene to deeper levels. Yuri Tsivian, for example, has proposed that the peacock represents the Winter Palace itself, which, adopting a sexual metaphor, Kerensky literally enters from behind.[23] To bolster his interpretation, Tsivian offers several other examples of visual metaphors deployed in *October* to equate the capturing of the Winter Palace with sexual conquest or even rape. What is important here is less the question of whether such interpretations are accepted or rejected than of the degree of complexity and ambiguity that Eisenstein's montage invites.

Among the more ambitious and, as it turned out, controversial metaphors deployed by Eisenstein are those signifying the threat to the Revolution during the July Days. As General Kornilov musters his forces to launch a monarchist, counter-Revolutionary attack, ordinary workers and soldiers arm themselves to defend the city while members of the Provisional

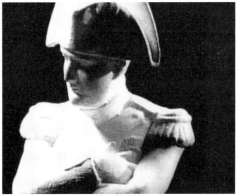

Government prevaricate within the safe and luxurious confines of
their new headquarters. Here, long shots of Kerensky are juxtaposed with close-ups showing a small figurine representing the
French Emperor Napoleon in an identical pose. By alluding to
Kerensky's Napoleonic tendencies, Eisenstein reinforces the
notion that the Revolution has been betrayed. To elaborate this
idea further, he juxtaposes a shot of Kornilov astride his horse
with a small equestrian statue, also representing Napoleon.
The 'two Napoleons' are then placed side by side to suggest
there is little to separate them.

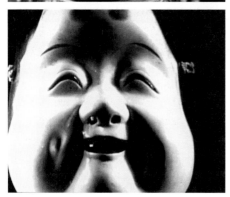

'For God and Country', *October*.

In these montage sequences, Eisenstein was striving to find a cinematic language consonant with linguistic expression. As he expressed it in an article published in *Kino* in March 1928,

> The sphere of the new film language will, as it happens, not be the sphere of the presentation of phenomena, nor even that of social interpretation, but the opportunity for *abstract social evaluation* . . . It will be the art of the direct cinematic communication of a slogan. Of communication that is just as unobstructed and immediate as the communication of an idea through a qualified word.[24]

Eisenstein took this emerging notion of 'intellectual' montage to its furthest point in what has come to be known as the 'For God and Country' sequence. Commencing with an inter-title quoting Kornilov's infamous slogan, Eisenstein sought, in purely visual terms, to deconstruct and demystify the very basis for religious belief. The sequence edits together a series of close-ups of representations of deities, initially presented alongside architectural details of religious buildings. First a Baroque statue of Christ in Majesty is interspersed with shots of the onion domes of the Cathedral of the Spilt Blood in Leningrad. This signifies Russian Orthodox Christianity. Next, in rapid succession, come shots of various Eastern deities, with details of a mosque interspersed. Here, though Eisenstein's choice of deity is not consistently authentic, is a suggestion of the continuing influence of broadly Eastern religions, particularly Islam, in the further reaches of Soviet territory. The sequence culminates in the representation of deities of early Asian and North American origin, concluding with simple, carved-wood figurines from Africa. As Eisenstein later pointed out, the sequence as a whole was intended to link contemporary religious belief with ancient, outmoded superstitions. In his own, admittedly problematic primitivizing language, 'these shots were assembled on a descending intellectual scale and lead the notion of god back to a block of wood.'[25]

Finally, *October* turns its attention to events immediately preceding the Revolution itself: Lenin's return to Petrograd, the defeat of the Mensheviks, the arming of the Revolutionary forces, Kerensky's flight to safety and the shots fired on the Winter Palace by the battleship *Aurora*. The most famous scene, the storming of the Winter Palace, brings the film to a resoundingly glorious conclusion as the masses take control of the palace and declare the birth of the first proletarian, socialist state. Once more *October* is deluged with symbolic and metaphorical references. For example, a Bolshevik sailor is shown single-handedly defending a bridge and turning back the advances of a multitude of, admittedly elderly, defenders of the Provisional Government. Here the notion that determination and self-sacrifice are inherent qualities of Bolshevism is reinforced by an allusion to Livy's ancient tale of Horatius defending the bridge. This both enhances and contextualizes the historical significance of the action.[26] In the final scenes, a young boy, symbolizing the future generations in whose name the Revolution has been won, sits astride the former Tsar's throne and waves his cap in glee as clocks, indicating the time throughout the world, take note of this key moment in history. With the victory of the Bolsheviks, time itself is transformed and the entire planet enters a new era.

The various delays in the completion of *October* generated a mounting sense of curiosity and anticipation among Soviet critics while its eventual release on the eve of the 1928 Party Conference generated a flurry of press responses. Reception, however, was at best muted. Some hailed Eisenstein's new work as a landmark in cinematic history. Pudovkin, for example, particularly praised Kerensky's 'ascension' scene, although, by his own admission, he had only seen separate sequences at the editing stage.[27] Lunacharsky highlighted 'the grandiose flood of astonishing, and sometimes even brilliant parts' in a film that left him with 'the impression of an enormous triumph'.[28] Yet lingering doubts seemed to hover over even these positive reactions. Indeed, it was the parts, rather than the whole, that seemed to please. Adrian Pyotrovsky, who had previously described *Potemkin* as nothing less than 'a masterpiece of Soviet film', best encapsulated this uncertainty when he described general reaction to *October* as 'admiration for the details of the film and a bewildered coolness towards the film as a whole'.[29] Retaining his earlier opinion that Eisenstein was indeed a 'brilliant master', he called for the film to be re-edited, presumably in the hope that reworking the material might result in an end product more akin to *Potemkin*.

Where Pyotrovsky was hesitant, others were more forthright. Brik, for example, condemned the 'distorted reality' imposed on the film by the director. He was equally critical of Eisenstein's use of cinematic metaphor, condemning what he saw as little more than 'the careless juxtaposition of objects and people'.[30] What really concerned the critics, however, was the question of how the public would engage with *October*. Viktor Shklovsky was one of the first to draw attention to this issue, writing, 'After viewing some Eisenstein sequences a man who is intelligent and conversant with cinema said to me, "That is very good. I like that a lot but what will the masses say? What will the people we are working for say?"'[31] The answer, as far as can be discerned, turned out to be at best ambivalent. T. Rokotov, for example, reported 'a loud sound of snoring' at a workers' club during a screening of *October* and, despite identifying Eisenstein as 'a most talented director', declared that the film was too 'difficult for a broad-based audience to understand'.[32] Eisenstein had been too self-indulgent, cerebral and obscure, and, in straying too far from conventional filmmaking, had risked losing the very audience for whom his films were ostensibly made. Rokotov's views largely reflected those expressed at the 1928 Party Conference. Here, the main conclusion was, that while cinema, as a whole, should 'not follow in the wake of the audience, but move ahead of it . . . instill into it new views, tastes, habits which correspond to the task of the socialist reconstruction of the whole of society', it should, at the same time, be 'intelligible to the millions'.[33] *October*, so it was argued, patently failed in this latter fundamental objective.

In January 1928, shortly after completing the first full version of *October*, Eisenstein switched his attention back to *The General Line*. Even as he set to work editing footage shot over a year previously, political events began to take a dramatic turn. The winter of 1927–8 witnessed a sharp decline in grain supplies, sparking fears of food shortages. Although this was a consequence of both a poor harvest and inadequate state planning, the blame was laid squarely at the feet of the peasants or, more accurately, a particular class of peasant. The kulak, or small land-holding peasant, was increasingly demonized as the arch-enemy of the state and the main obstacle to progress in the countryside. Demands for a more rigorous approach to collectivization began to creep up the political agenda. Thus, when Eisenstein showed a rough cut of *The General Line* to the authorities, its affinities with the gradualism of the Fourteenth Party Congress were seen to reflect an outdated policy. Stalin had already begun to impose emergency measures, sending troops into the countryside to appropriate supplies.

Over the next few months, Eisenstein wrote a new script and once more set out to film in the countryside. By February 1929, the film was finally ready for release, and, in anticipation of the premiere, Eisenstein and Alexandrov published an article in the journal *Sovetskii Ekran*. The title, 'An Experiment Intelligible to the Millions', suggested just how much of an impact both the 1928 Party Conference and critical reactions to *October* had made. Distancing themselves from what had been regarded as the earlier film's greatest failures, the authors declared:

The General Line does not glitter with mass meetings. It does not trumpet fanfares of formal discoveries. It does not flabbergast people with puzzling stunts.

It tells of humdrum everyday, but nonetheless profound, collaboration: the town and the countryside, the state farm and the collective farm, the *muzhik* [peasant] and the machine, the horse and the tractor – on the difficult path to a single goal.

Like that path, the film must be clear, simple and intelligible.[34]

Eisenstein, it seemed, had been both humbled and tamed. Yet, in a typically robust, even confrontational flourish, the article concluded that, 'while rejecting the glitter of external formal searches and whims, [the film] is inescapably an experiment. May this experiment, however contradictory it may sound, be an *experiment intelligible to the millions!*'[35] Eisenstein was fully aware that the introduction of this latter phrase, in the context of contemporary debates, was nothing less than an oxymoron, 'experimental' and 'intelligible' cinema being regarded as polar opposites. Once again, he was deploying conventional Marxist dialectics to suggest that his current work was resolving contemporary tensions and thus raising Soviet cinematography to a new, exalted level. As things turned out, however, few critics would concur on this point.

With final preparations for the premiere under way, Eisenstein was to be delivered yet another blow. In early April, Stalin viewed the film and afterwards asked to see both him and Alexandrov. Reportedly, Stalin felt that the conclusion to the film did not sufficiently reflect the dynamic change now demanded of the countryside. A new ending would have to be appended. Stalin's intervention is of much interest here. Doubtless, the Soviet leader saw the need for an ending in keeping with contemporary political imperatives. However, as Vance Kepley has suggested, he may well also have been adopting a delaying tactic.[36] By demanding that new footage be shot and edited, the film's release was held up until

October 1929, by which time the launch of Stalin's new policy of mass collectivization was imminent. Indeed, as Kepley has further pointed out, the release date was planned to coincide with the celebration of 'Collectivization Day' in October 1929, and, contrary to usual practice, Eisenstein's movie was released not just in Moscow, but concurrently in 52 cities throughout the Soviet Union, thus ensuring a wide audience.[37] Finally, to reinforce the more dynamic and staunchly class-oppositional political shift, the title was also changed. *The General Line* became *The Old and the New*.

Although described as a rural tale in six parts, *The Old and the New* might more usefully be divided into a prologue and three acts, each part structured around the natural cycle of the seasons. The film commences in the last throes of winter, represented by the interior of a dark, squalid peasant hut in which people and animals are shown living cheek by jowl. Lulled into a state of virtual hibernation by the soporific and suffocating fumes of a fire, these peasants represent the stagnant paralysis of the mass of peasants who, as the inter-titles inform us, remain 'illiterate, uneducated, backward'. To highlight this notional ignorance, the movie focuses on the absurd actions of two peasant brothers who deal with their dual inheritance by sawing their farmhouse in two. Greed and ignorance, the film argues, lead to the division of land and property and, subsequently, inefficient agricultural practices. To reinforce further the absurdity of this division, fences are being erected across the land, slicing it into ever smaller, unworkable plots.

Spring, however, is imminent, and with the change of season come the first signs of hope, here personified by the peasant woman Marfa Lapkina. *The Old and the New* was the first of Eisenstein's films in which plot is built around a single character, the archetypal positive heroine. Starting out as a downtrodden victim of the kulaks, Lapkina embarks on a journey of self-discovery and enlightenment, emerging at the end of the film as a modern, liberated individual who has thrown off the shackles of her peasant past. This focus on

'Marfa Lapkina Seated on the Earth', *The Old and the New*, 1929.

Lapkina's transformation, literally into a Soviet new woman, reflects
contemporary concerns, not least the broad debates, focused on the
role of women in Soviet society. In 1919, for example, the formation
of an official women's organization, known as the Zhenotdel, reflected the desire to improve conditions for women and to fight for
greater equality. A key objective here was to give women greater
financial independence by bringing them into the labour force,
though it might be added that the demographic decline in the young
male population in the wake of the First World War and the Civil
War also necessitated an increased mobilization of female workers.
Eisenstein's film aptly articulates the ambiguities of gender politics
of the mid- to late 1920s. Thus, while Lapkina achieves an increased
level of independence, authority and respect, this remains predicated
upon her status as a worker, an economic resource of the state.
Further, her subservience to male political authority, most notably in

the figure of the Agricultural Commissar (who bears a remarkable physical resemblance to Lenin), is maintained throughout the film. In this context, Lapkina might be read as a blueprint for much Soviet literature and cinema produced over the next decade.

Yet, Lapkina is much more than simply an archetypal Soviet heroine. For example, Eisenstein also adopts a conventional literary trope, inspired by his reading of Emile Zola's *La Terre* (1887), and presents Lapkina as a cipher for nature. When she is first introduced she is shown squatting on the bare earth, as if she has emerged from the very soil itself. As she raises her face to the camera, her rugged, careworn physiognomy echoes the parched and windswept landscape that surrounds her. Here she can be read as a metaphorical, if somewhat clichéd, 'Mother Russia'. Yet Eisenstein takes the metaphor further. Much as the land relies on the sun to regenerate itself, Lapkina too draws her strength and energy from the first rays of the spring sunshine, and, from this point on, the sun occupies an increasingly vital role within the overall narrative.[38] Initially, Lapkina, like the rest of the peasants, is overwhelmed by the relentless heat of the sun. Forced to work her land using only a traditional wooden plough pulled by an emaciated cow, she soon realizes the impossibility of the task before her. Rather than succumb to defeat, however, she raises her fists to the air and rails against the social injustice that has brought her so low. This is the key transitional moment in the plot, as Lapkina is transformed from oppressed, victimized peasant to purposeful individual taking control of her own destiny. To signify this shift, Eisenstein cuts back and forth from shots of Lapkina in the field to Lapkina standing on a platform making a political speech demanding collectivization. However, it is not just a spatial and temporal shift that occurs here. Rather, Lapkina's very relationship to the sun is altered. In the field she is shot from a low angle, backlit by the bright sky, her face in shadow. On the political stage she is shot from a similarly low angle, once again backlit by a bright sky. Now,

'Marfa Lapkina Illuminated', *The Old and the New*.

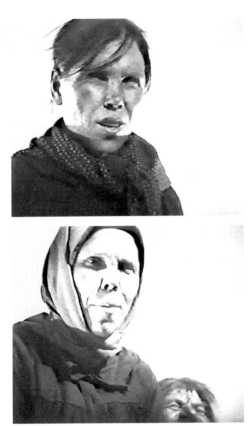

however, her face is fully illuminated. As the shots switch back and forth, Lapkina's moment of conversion is articulated as a transition from darkness to light. She no longer fights against the power of the sun, but rather embraces this ultimate source of energy and productivity, reflecting it outwards towards those peasants yet to be enlightened.

At several points throughout the film Eisenstein reiterates Lapkina's capacity to harness the power of the sun and cast its glow upon those around her. For example, when she, alone among the local peasant community, joins forces with a young member of the Communist League to establish a dairy collective, she is shown slowly turning her face towards her new comrade. As her gaze falls on the youngster, he is similarly illuminated, causing him to screw up his eyes against the overwhelming glow emanating from Lapkina.[39] In this way, her decision to join forces with the collectivization plan advocated by the state is presented as equivalent to joining forces with the ultimate and irrepressible power of nature itself.

The sun also plays a key role in the next scene, in which Lapkina's new-found enlightenment is starkly contrasted with the unenlightened peasants who continue to cling to old ways. As spring turns to summer, a drought ensues, threatening the livelihood of the local community. In a panic, many of the peasants turn to religion, calling upon God to relieve their suffering and bring rain. They organize a church procession and, in a scene derived from Ilya Repin's painting *Easter Procession in Kursk* (1880–83), Eisenstein contrasts Lapkina's rational faith in Bolshevism with the superstitions and rituals of the Orthodox Church. To suggest the uncritical, herd-like mentality of peasant religiosity, Eisenstein intersplices close-ups of the peasants crossing themselves with shots of bleating sheep. As a dark cloud gathers overhead, the peasants throw themselves to the ground in further supplication, believing momentarily that their prayers have been answered. The cloud, however, passes overhead releasing not a single drop of rain. One of the priests, now glancing anxiously at the sky, pulls out a barometer surreptitiously concealed beneath his vestments. As he taps it with his finger, the light falls to reveal the French words '*très sec*' ('very dry'). One by one the peasants slowly rise and drift away, disappointed.

The Church's failure to achieve a miracle is now contrasted with the capacity of rational science to bring about seemingly miraculous transformations. Lapkina's collective has taken possession of a new machine, a cream separator that facilitates the production of butter. As the machine is unveiled to the local peasant community, this too emanates a reflective light symbolic of its potential to enlighten the masses. At first, the peasants remain sceptical as the handle of the new-fangled separator is turned. Following the principles devised for the Odessa-steps sequence in *Potemkin*, Eisenstein now builds the tension by accelerating the editing process, intercutting close-ups and longer shots until tension is released as the machine explodes in an orgasmic fashion, showering Lapkina in a white, sticky foam. For Eisenstein, however, this ecstatic moment signified far more than an allusion to sexual release. His concept of 'ecstasy' referred back to the original meaning of the word derived from the Greek '*ex-stasis*', or 'beyond the body'. In this context, the attempt to induce an ecstatic condition in the spectator can be equated to Eisenstein's earlier notion, outlined in 'The Montage of Attractions', that the purpose of cinema is not to entertain, nor even simply to educate, but, more radically, to effect the transformation of the very consciousness of the audience. To reinforce this concept, the ecstatic moment within the cream-separator sequence in *The Old and the New* results immediately in a dramatic shift of consciousness, and indeed behaviour, among the watching peasants. From this point onwards, membership of the collective grows exponentially, and the dairy is officially declared a success.

Despite this early victory, Lapkina is forced to overcome yet more obstacles on her metaphorical journey from unreformed peasant to Soviet new woman. Next she challenges the greed of the peasants when they seek to divide the profits from the cream separator. With the support of the Agricultural Commissar, Lapkina persuades the collective to invest the income and sets off on a journey to a modern state-run farm, or Sovkhoz, to purchase a bull. In the subsequent scene, Eisenstein consciously disrupts the spectator's sense of temporal specificity, collapsing present and future. On arrival at the Sovkhoz, Lapkina is overwhelmed by the sight of this modern agricultural enterprise, part factory and part scientific laboratory. Indeed, she goes so far as to doubt her own eyes, believing that what she sees is a dream. In effect, she is here given a utopian vision of the future, yet one that exists in the present. Notably, this collapsing of contemporary reality with utopian future presages one of the main principles of Socialist Realism, officially introduced as the exclusive method for depicting Soviet culture five years later. Lapkina's glimpse of the future in the present thus reiterates one of the main themes explored in *The Old and the New*, namely the crossing, or transgressing, of boundaries. Intriguingly, Eisenstein employed the modernist architect Andrei Burov to build the set for this scene. The white-stuccoed, band-windowed, modernist villa makes a clear reference to the work of Le Corbusier at the very time that the Swiss architect was working on the Tsentrosoyuz building on Myasnitskaya Ulitsa in Moscow, just around the corner from Eisenstein's Chistye Prudy flat.

On her return to the collective, Lapkina is soon brought back down to earth by the pressing need to modernize. As summer turns to autumn, bad weather delays the harvest, highlighting the need for a tractor to secure the threatened crops. Yet, once more, Lapkina encounters obstacles, this time in the form of official bureaucracy as the collective's request for a tractor is rejected out of hand in a long-winded letter composed in excessively obfuscatory language. To signify the absurdity of this communication, Eisenstein focuses on the over-elaborate signature of the head bureaucrat, its swirls, curlicues and underlinings occupying virtually half a page. For Eisenstein, this excess of decoration signifies both the self aggrandizement of bureaucrats and an inability to focus effort in the right places.

One of the most effective ways in which *The Old and the New* parodies bureaucracy, however, is in Tisse's use of a wide-angle lens. The 'machines of bureaucracy' – the typewriter, the pencil sharpener and banks of telephones – are all shot from low angles and in close-up, making them appear monumental and dwarfing the office staff operating them. In this configuration they also appear as

'The Machines of Bureaucracy', *The Old and the New*.

impenetrable barriers behind which bureaucracy hides from the
demands of the real world, thus reiterating the significance of
boundaries and the need to transgress them in the name of progress. Eisenstein's attack on excessive bureaucracy was entirely in
keeping with official Soviet policy. Indeed, Lenin himself had earlier
warned of the dangers of bureaucratic structures inhibiting the
direct action required of a dynamic revolution. Yet, this overt
critique was almost certainly double-edged, Eisenstein here taking
a sideswipe at the increase in bureaucracy within the film industry
and the impositions that this inevitably made upon his own work.

Through sheer determination, willpower and resistance to such
bureaucratic stagnation, Lapkina finally secures a tractor which is
duly unveiled to the collective at a grand ceremony reminiscent
of the earlier religious procession. An urban driver has even been
drafted in to operate the new machine, once again establishing a link

'Tractors', *The Old and the New*.

between town and country. After a false start, the tractor is revealed to be a marvel of the modern age as it ploughs its way across the landscape, driving straight through the fences erected at the beginning of the film. Thus, both literally and metaphorically, modernization breaks down the last barriers against collectivization. In an interesting twist, the tractor is then turned directly towards the camera and, in a scene reminiscent of the final shot of *Potemkin*, is driven directly towards the screen and thus the audience. Is Eisenstein here suggesting that any recalcitrance still evident among viewers of the movie will similarly be crushed?

Finally, Eisenstein introduces one of the most striking scenes in the whole film. As the camera cuts to a long shot, dozens of tractors enter a field to perform what can only be described as a choreographed dance that would not look out of place in a Red Square parade or, for that matter, a Busby Berkeley spectacular.

Moving in close synchronization, the tractors carve ever-increasing concentric circles into the land, signifying both the completion of the natural cycle and the expansive nature of the collectivization programme. Shots of ploughed land cut to shots of fully ripened wheat fields, which in turn cut to shots of grain silos full to brimming. The tractor, symbol of modernity, industrialization and collectivization, has thus transformed the countryside and secured the supply of food to the entire nation. This wider political message is now mapped directly back onto Lapkina herself. In an ironic pastiche of the ending to Chaplin's *A Woman of Paris* (1923), the urban tractor driver is shown wearing a peasant shirt and riding in the back of a hay wagon. As he passes a tractor coming in the opposite direction, he stops to greet the unknown driver, dressed from head to toe in a leather outfit more typical for a pilot. As the two face each other, the wagon driver, and we as spectators, gradually recognize that the tractor driver is none other than Lapkina, her wide, toothy grin instantly recognizable. As she removes her goggles and helmet we see that her entire appearance has altered, her hair elegantly tied back and her face carefully made up. Lapkina has completed her transformation into a Soviet new woman. As she, in urban dress, faces the former urbanite now in a peasant shirt, the division between city and country is presented as irrevocably broken, and the scene effectively becomes a manifestation of Stalin's speech at the 1929 Conference of Marxian Agrarians:

The question of the relations between the town and the village is assuming a new footing, and the effacement of the contrast between the town and the village will be accelerated.

This circumstance, comrades, is of the utmost importance for our construction. It will transform the psychology of the peasant and will turn him towards the town . . . It will make it possible to supplement the slogan of the Party 'face to the village' by the slogan for the collective farm peasant 'face to the town'.[40]

The metaphorical transition from darkness to light that characterizes Lapkina's journey, and thus that of the entire Soviet nation, might also be applied to Eisenstein's own transition from *October* to *The Old and the New*, for while both films deploy metaphor and symbolism, they remain strikingly distinctive products. Perhaps most significantly, *The Old and the New* is a much lighter film than *October*, in more than one sense of the word. It is, for example, quite literally flooded with light, with most scenes shot in the open air and in broad daylight. This marks a notable contrast with the darker, more louring quality of *October*, staged predominantly at night or indoors. Indeed in retrospect one wonders whether the general sense of obscurity ascribed to *October* by some critics might, at least in part, have derived from the overall sombre lighting effects.

The Old and the New is also lighter in mood despite the seriousness of the subject matter. In the wake of the criticisms levelled against *October*, there can be little doubt that Eisenstein strove to make a more accessible movie, even if he refused to relinquish the rich vein of metaphorical associations that underpin both the overall plot and individual scenes. Here, consideration should perhaps be given to contemporary debates concerning the development of Soviet comedy. As Denise Youngblood has claimed, more was written about comedy than any other genre in the late 1920s, and 'critics were constantly declaring comedy the most important genre of the most important art'.[41] In *The Old and the New*, Eisenstein deployed comedy more openly and extensively than in his previous two films, as might be discerned from the absurdity of the peasant brothers sawing their own farmhouse in half, or the extensive use of caricature for negative characters, such as the corpulent and overly decorous kulak couple who refuse to lend Lapkina a horse, and the excessively pedantic bureaucrats. This comedic dimension is also evident in the scene of the ritual wedding of a cow and a bull, culminating in a speeded-up sequence showing a bull quivering with anticipation as it races towards the rear end of a somewhat nervous looking cow in order to 'consummate the marriage'. Despite the obvious reference to productivity, this scene seems designed explicitly to elicit laughter more than serious contemplation, as well as offering a spoof on the excessive emphasis on romance in Hollywood movies. Indeed it is difficult to imagine contemporary spectators regarding it as anything other than a slightly risqué comic interlude.

The comedic is also much in evidence in the penultimate sequence of the film in which the tractor tows a train of wagons across the open fields chased by peasants on horseback. Here the double reference, firstly to a convoy of wagons, secondly to a train, crossing the frontiers of the Wild West pursued by armed and angry Native Americans, provides a clear pastiche of the Hollywood western.[42] Yet, once more, even this comedic reference carries wider connotations, as the Russian landscape becomes a space to be tamed and colonized through the process of collectivization much as the American frontier was colonized under the aegis of 'Manifest Destiny'. And there can be little doubt as to who represents the cowboys and who the 'injuns'.

Ultimately, Eisenstein's emphasis on comedy in *The Old and the New* seems closer in mood to his first movie, *Strike*, while its extensive metaphorical richness derives more directly from his cinematic experiments in both *Potemkin* and *October*. Its importance, therefore, lies in its synthesis of the sheer breadth of cinematic ideas he had been developing up to this point. As things turned out, *The Old and the New* would also be the last major production completed by Eisenstein for the best part of the decade to come. His next proposal, to produce a film version of nothing less than Marx's *Das Kapital*, was held to be overly ambitious even by the most politically conscious members of the Bolshevik regime and failed to gain the support of Sovkino. Indeed, his career as a filmmaker now entered something of a hiatus.

4

Hiatus

In August 1928, Joseph Schenk, the Russian-born president of United Artists, visited Moscow, where he met Eisenstein and reconfirmed the Fairbanks and Pickford invitation to work in Hollywood. For some time, Eisenstein had been keen to visit the cinema capital of the world, but commitments to complete both *October* and *The Old and the New* had precluded the possibility of his leaving the Soviet Union. In the autumn of 1929, however, with no new commissions on the horizon, he gained official permission to travel to the United States, his mission being to study recent developments in film technology, specifically the advent of sound.

Less than two years earlier, on 6 October 1927, Warner's Theatre in New York had hosted the premiere of the first commercially released, feature-length sound movie, *The Jazz Singer*. Although far from being the first experiment successfully synchronizing sound and image – demonstrations of short sound films had taken place in both New York and Berlin at least five years earlier – *The Jazz Singer* soon became the catalyst for the expansion of the new technology. Over the following year, Hollywood's major film studios switched entirely to sound production while cinemas were rapidly equipped to facilitate the screening of the wondrous 'talking pictures'. In Europe, too, sound technology developed rapidly so that towards the end of 1929, when Eisenstein's *The Old and the New* first reached the Continent, silent films were already beginning to look like the product of a past era.

Eisenstein had anticipated the impact that the advent of sound would have on cinematography. In the summer of 1928, for example, he issued an official 'Statement on Sound', co-signed by Alexandrov and Pudovkin and published not only in the Soviet Union but also in Germany and Great Britain. He and his colleagues saw enormous potential in sound cinema. However, they also expressed a worry that 'attempts are being made to use this new improvement in cinema for the wrong purposes.'[1] The principal fear was that sound would be used to produce 'photographed presentations of a theatrical order', thus diminishing the importance of cinema as an autonomous medium.[2] Rather than simply making 'talking pictures', Eisenstein and his fellow writers advocated a new development of montage techniques that would result in 'the creation of a new *orchestral counterpoint* of visual and sound images'.[3] He would further develop this notion of 'contrapuntal sound' in his next article, 'An Unexpected Juncture'.[4] Returning to his early passion for all things Japanese, he linked the recent performances in Moscow of a touring Kabuki troupe with his developing ideas about sound film. For Eisenstein, what made Kabuki so special was not its use of image and sound, but its total integration of these dual aspects of performance. 'Instead of accompaniment,' he wrote, 'the Kabuki reveals the method of transference: the transference of the basic affective intention from one material to another, from one category of "stimulant" to another.'[5] Notably, he saw the Kabuki experience as approaching the condition of synaesthesia, in which one type of stimulation had the capacity to evoke the sensation of another: 'We actually "hear movement" and "see sound".'[6] What was most important for Eisenstein was the notion that sound and image ought not to be independent entities but rather co-dependent constituents generating a whole greater than the sum of its parts. Thus, the development of sound cinema offered enormous potential for an interaction between the visual and the aural, and this would once more raise the cinematic medium to a higher plain. However, Eisenstein faced one major problem. As he openly acknowledged, 'We who work in the USSR recognize that, given our technical capabilities, the practical implementation of sound cinema is not feasible in the near future.'[7] With neither the technical expertise nor the hard currency to import the necessary equipment, the prospects for the Soviet Union developing its own sound cinema looked fairly bleak. The opportunity to work in Hollywood would, Eisenstein believed, potentially rectify this shortcoming.

In late August 1929, Eisenstein, Alexandrov and Tisse boarded a train bound for Berlin, where they planned to attend the premiere of *The Old and the New* before securing visas for entry into the United States. As the Soviet authorities had supplied them with just $25 each in cash, they knew they would have to find work to support themselves throughout the trip. They were probably less aware that it would be nearly three years before they would again set foot on Soviet soil.

Once in Berlin, Eisenstein attended as many screenings of sound films as he could, mostly popular Hollywood productions.[8] His first major European undertaking, however, was to attend the International Congress of Independent Film Makers at the chateau of Mme Hélène de Mandrot in La Sarraz, Switzerland. Here Eisenstein was introduced to many of Europe's best-known avant-garde filmmakers, including Hans Richter, Walter Ruttmann and Alberto Cavalcanti. He also saw films by Man Ray, Viking Eggeling and Luis Buñuel. There was, perhaps, a sense of irony in Eisenstein's attendance at this congress, not least as his attitudes towards filmmaking diverged significantly from many of those among this august company who valued his work more for its aesthetic qualities than for its desire to revolutionize the masses. Further, given his status as a big studio director now seeking to make his name in Hollywood, he was not entirely in tune with the primary objective of the congress, namely to establish a collective

Sergei Eisenstein, (left) with Léon Moussinac at La Sarraz, Switzerland, 1929.

to facilitate the production and distribution of independent films. Eisenstein and his Soviet colleagues picked up on this tension and suggested making a spoof allegory pitting independent cinema against its commercial rival. Shot in one day, and featuring most of the delegates in costumes appropriated from Mme de Mandrot's chateau, the film was never edited and was subsequently lost, though some still photographs remain extant.

After the congress, Eisenstein spent an additional fortnight in Switzerland, during which time he gave several lectures in Zurich and also participated in the making of a public-information film entitled *Women's Misery – Women's Joy*. This short production, part melodrama, part documentary, highlighted the dangers of back-street abortions, contrasting the squalid, unhygienic nature of such illegal practices with the pristine, scientifically monitored conditions in an officially sanctioned gynaecological clinic in Zurich. Here, the somewhat clichéd comparison of good and bad practices, presented as light versus dark, order versus disorder, and modern science versus old ways, is reminiscent of the visual style deployed in posters of the early Bolshevik era. Later, Eisenstein would deny responsibility for this film despite being officially credited as its director. Economic necessity, rather than artistic aspiration, appears to have been the main driving force behind his decision to participate in the production.

Back in Berlin, Eisenstein was introduced to many of the city's most influential cultural figures, including the playwrights Ernst Toller and Luigi Pirandello, the stage director Erwin Piscator and the artist George Grosz. Among other influential Berlin luminaries, he spent much time with the eminent psychoanalyst Dr Hanns Sachs and lectured at the Berlin Psychoanalytical Institute.[9] He was also reacquainted with the dancer Valeska Gert, whom he had previously met in Moscow. Together they spent much time at the fashionable Romantisches Café and in the more exotic clubs and cafés of the Weimar capital.

During his early career, Eisenstein had often benefited from propitious timing in his projects. Now, however, things began to work against him. In October 1929, the Wall Street Crash threw the American economy into turmoil, resulting in the major Hollywood studios adopting a far more cautious attitude to investment in risky propositions. More troublingly, the United Artists invitation was withdrawn, and Eisenstein's chances of getting to Hollywood began to look more and more remote. Unwilling to abandon his long-term goal, he took up a host of offers to prolong his stay in Europe. In November he attended a private screening of *Potemkin* in London, still officially banned in the UK. Having been invited by Ivor Montagu, the founder of the London Film Society whom he had earlier met at La Sarraz, he delivered a series of lectures in a room

A landscape in *Romance sentimentale*, 1930.

above Foyle's bookshop on Charing Cross Road. He was also introduced to George Bernard Shaw, who offered him the film rights to
Arms and the Man (1894). Eisenstein never took up the offer.

By early December the Soviet director had moved to Paris,
where he met James Joyce. A long-time fan of *Ulysses* (1922),
Eisenstein discussed the concept of the inner monologue with the
ageing, now nearly blind, author, who later declared that only
Eisenstein or Ruttmann could have turned this infamous publication
into a film.[10] A few days later Eisenstein returned to England, where
he delivered a lecture at Cambridge and participated in an avant-
garde film Richter was making at the London Film Society. For his
part, Eisenstein donned the costume of a British policeman and
performed 'a ballet of the bobby on point duty'.[11] With his typical
linguistic flair he was comically juxtaposing the French term for
dancing *en pointe* with the English term for controlling traffic.

In late December, Eisenstein returned to Paris. It was now four
months since he had left Moscow; he had achieved no experience
of sound cinema, and the prospect of reaching Hollywood seemed

more distant than ever. At this point, however, an unexpected opportunity presented itself. In Eisenstein's absence, Alexandrov had been introduced to the wealthy Parisian jeweller Léonard Rosenthal, who was looking for someone to shoot a short promotional film for his mistress, the Russian émigrée and aspiring singer/actress Mara Gris. As finances for the project would not be in short supply, Eisenstein, Alexandrov and Tisse willingly agreed to take on the commission. The result was a twenty-minute sound movie entitled *Romance sentimentale*.

Described in the opening titles as a *'vieille romance russe'*, *Romance sentimentale* is an elegy, far more concerned with mood than narrative.[12] As the title credits fade, the camera zooms in on waves crashing violently against a shore and storm-battered trees swaying recklessly or tumbling to the ground, the whole set against a background of dark, dramatic music. Here, the raw power of nature is introduced metaphorically to signify the emotional turmoil of Mara Gris. However, as the storm slowly subsides, the musical energy also diminishes, and attention shifts to gently scintillating reflections on the surface of calm waters. This more contemplative mood is augmented as the camera pans out to show a tranquil, Impressionist-inspired landscape, reminiscent of Claude Monet's series of paintings of poplar trees. Next, the scene shifts to an elaborate domestic interior with long, lingering shots of Gris silhouetted against a window. The low-lit, empty space of the room, gently ticking clock and accompanying melody in a minor key all evoke a melancholy mood. As Gris sits at a piano, she begins to sing a doleful Russian melody that further emphasizes a sense of nostalgia for a lost world. At this point, however, a more experimental cinematic element is introduced. As the music again rises to a crescendo, a series of small starburst explosions fills the screen. These, as Eisenstein acknowledged, were created by scratching the surface of the film with a pen.[13] Following his principle of ecstasy as ex-stasis, literally a leaving of the body, Gris is now transported out of her melancholic

'Rodin's *The Kiss*', *Romance sentimentale*.

world (and mood) into the heavens, where she sits at a gleaming white grand piano, surrounded by clouds. Shots of graceful white swans swimming elegantly in the still waters of a lake are interspersed with close-up, soft-focus shots of figurative sculptures, the works of Auguste Rodin, which, through careful editing, perform a cinematic dance accompanied by fireworks exploding in the sky. As the music reaches its climax, three rapidly edited shots of Rodin's *The Kiss* (*c.* 1880s) move from the vertical to the horizontal, an erotic reworking of the Alupka lions sequence from *Potemkin*. The ecstatic moment having past, however, the music returns to a minor key, and Gris is transported back to her oppressive, melancholic present. The film does not end on this pessimistic note, however; the spectator is brought out into the open air as spring arrives and trees burst into blossom. Gris is again seated at a white piano, a broad smile on her face as the wind caresses her hair and a flock of white doves flies into the blue yonder.

It is perhaps not surprising that *Romance sentimentale* has frequently been dismissed, or given only a fleeting mention, by Eisenstein scholars. Certainly the strong emphasis on melancholy and nostalgia sits rather awkwardly alongside his earlier productions. Moreover, his later claims that he played only a minor role in the production has led to speculation that the movie is far more reflective of Alexandrov's work than Eisenstein's. It must be admitted that *Romance sentimentale* bears some of the hallmarks of Alexandrov's later, Hollywood-style musical comedies, such as *The Happy Guys* (1934) and *Volga-Volga* (1938). However, as Oksana Bulgakowa has pointed out, in a letter sent to his secretary and close confidant Pera Atasheva, Eisenstein acknowledged a far greater participation than has often been assumed, even describing, with great enthusiasm, the 'remarkable results' of his first practical experience in making a sound film.[14]

Yet perhaps what has made most Eisenstein scholars reluctant to engage with *Romance sentimentale* is its highly problematic political message. Given Gris's aristocratic bearing and known status as a member of the Russian ex-patriot community, many of whom had fled Russia after the Revolution, it is difficult to conclude that her nostalgia is for anything other than the good old days under the Tsar. More troubling still, her spring-time emergence from a melancholy reverie would seem to imply a cyclical return to the splendours of the pre-Revolutionary era after a dark and stormy, but mercifully brief, Bolshevik winter, and there can be little doubt that both Rosenthal and Gris would have approved of this message. For a team of committed Soviet filmmakers, however, it was at best ambiguous, at worst disingenuous. Indeed it is tempting to surmise that it was the politics, as much as the aesthetics, of *Romance sentimentale*, that contributed to Eisenstein's decision to distance himself from the production. The film's relatively poor critical reception was probably a further contributing factor. In the end, his participation did provide him with vitally important income and an opportunity to experiment with sound as an integral aspect of his developing montage techniques. Ultimately, however, it did little to enhance his career or reputation.

Having moved to the Hôtel des Etats-Unis on Avenue Montparnasse, Eisenstein now became a regular at the café haunts of Paris's cultural élite – La Coupole, Le Dôme and Les Deux Magots – where he met the cream of the city's cultural community. Among those to whom he was introduced were the writers Tristan Tzara, Louis Aragon, Robert Desnos, Paul Éluard and André Malraux; the artists André Derain and Max Ernst; and the avant-garde filmmakers Fernand Léger – best known in cinema circles for his animated avant-garde production *Ballet mécanique* (1924) – and Jean Cocteau, at the time working on his first film, *Le Sang d'un poète* (1930). Eisenstein also became acquainted with Colette and spent much time driving around Paris with her stepson in a blue Bugatti, a fact that doubtless diminished his Communist credentials in the eyes of many.[15] His meeting with Filippo Marinetti, the controversial founder of Italian Futurism, was less conducive to social harmony. As Marinetti was now a close political ally of Mussolini, the newspapers made much sport of the encounter between 'one of the prophets of Fascism' and 'one of Communism's angry disciples'.[16] Other key figures in the Parisian art world introduced to Eisenstein included the photographers André Kertesz, Germaine Krull and Eli Lotar. The cabaret artiste, model and painter Alice Prin, better known as Kiki de Montparnasse, even produced a portrait of the Soviet director. Here, the rather serious-looking Eisenstein, posed against a simple backdrop of sea and sky in a style reminiscent of Russian icon painting, stares directly out at the viewer. On the right horizon, the dark outline of a steamship (the *Potemkin*, no doubt) looms menacingly forward, simultaneously acting to assist the identification of the sitter and as a signifier of Eisenstein's cultural 'invasion' of Europe.

Kiki de Montparnasse (Alice Prin), *Sergei Eisenstein*, 1929.

In February, Eisenstein visited the Joinville studios on the out-skirts of Paris, where he met Abel Gance, the director of the epic *Napoléon* (1927). As Gance was working on his first sound film, the science-fiction extravaganza *The End of the World*, the visit allowed Eisenstein to see a sound studio in action. He also discussed film projects with the famous Russian opera singer Fyodor Chaliapin and the French cabaret star Yvette Guilbert, but lack of funds prevented these projects from getting off the ground.

Throughout this time, Eisenstein's presence in Paris had been steadily attracting negative press attention as anti-Communist groups gained ever greater prominence in French politics. This was brought to a head in January 1930 when General Alexander Kutepov, a former member of the Russian White Army and leader of an exiled counter-Revolutionary group pledged to the restoration of the Tsarist monarchy, suddenly disappeared from his Paris apartment. All the evidence pointed to his having been kidnapped and killed by Soviet agents. This soon led to political turmoil as Paris's Russian émigré community staged violent protests outside the Soviet Embassy on the Rue de Grenelle. As Eisenstein himself later explained, the walls alongside the embassy were covered with posters and slogans declaiming, 'Throw the Soviets out of Paris!' and 'Run them out of town', while the French newspapers were 'filled with anti-Soviet shrieks'.[17] In the midst of this political crisis, Eisenstein was invited to the Sorbonne to introduce a screening of *The Old and the New*. Although the event was planned as invitation only, a large crowd gathered, some expressing support for the direc-tor, others vociferous opposition. Tensions were further heightened when the police arrived and demanded that the screening be can-celled on the grounds that *The Old and the New* had not been passed by the censors for public exhibition. With a huge and potentially volatile audience already in the hall, Eisenstein agreed to give an impromptu talk, though he must surely have been aware that this would be read as a clear political provocation. Recalling the event in later years, he wrote of his glowing triumph on this occasion, of an audience 'held captive, stunned by this foreigner, who had arrived, moreover, from a country considered for some reason to be irrationally authoritarian and quite devoid of any sense of humour'.[18] Whether or not this is an accurate reflection of the evening, the incident generated a major row, attracting press coverage in both France and the Soviet Union.[19] More problematically, the next morning police arrived at Eisenstein's hotel and took him in for questioning. As his visa was due to expire, his request for an extension was refused. He had, by now, become persona non grata in France.

Over the next few weeks, having managed to obtain minor extensions to his visa, Eisenstein redoubled his efforts to secure passage to Hollywood, fearing that expulsion from France might precipitate a call to return to the Soviet Union. In late April 1930, he finally received a telephone call from Jesse L. Lasky, head of Paramount Pictures, offering him a deal that would take him to Hollywood. Thrilled by this turn of events, Eisenstein hastily secured the permission of the Soviet authorities to travel to the United States. In early May, together with Tisse, he boarded the *Europa* and set sail for the New World. Alexandrov would follow shortly afterwards.

Eisenstein's arrival in New York was accompanied by a wave of publicity. Official lunches and press conferences were staged, followed by lectures at both Columbia and Harvard universities, all of which served to keep Paramount's newest acquisition very much in the public eye. This publicity, however, also drew some unwanted attention as Hollywood's political right launched a virulent anti-Bolshevik and anti-Semitic attack on Eisenstein. The leader of the campaign, Major Frank Pease, described the Soviet director as nothing less than a 'cut-throat red dog', part of a Jewish–Bolshevik conspiracy aiming to 'turn the American cinema into a communist cesspool'.[20] He even distributed a 24-page document titled 'Eisenstein, Hollywood's Messenger from Hell'. Although Paramount

Boris Efimov, 'A Great Victory for Democratic France'. The caption reads: 'The Expulsion of the Film Director Eisenstein from Paris.' Published in *Izvestiya*, 1930.

Крупная победа демократической Франции.

Рис. Бор. Ефимов.

ВЫСЫЛКА КИНОРЕЖИССЕРА ЭЙЗЕНШТЕЙНА ИЗ ПАРИЖА.

was swift to rebuff Pease's diatribes, the campaign nonetheless succeeded in deflecting attention from Eisenstein's artistic credentials, making him, once more, a focal point for political debate.

In the meantime, he and his colleagues set off for Los Angeles by train, arriving in June. As the Paramount contract ensured Eisenstein's group the princely sum of $900 a week, they took up residence in a large villa in Beverley Hills, complete with swimming pool, a DeSoto car and servants. Here they were joined by Ivor Montagu, who had been instrumental in securing Eisenstein's

Hollywood contract, and his wife Eileen, affectionately nicknamed 'Hell'. Once settled, Eisenstein sought out the town's most influential society, meeting, among others, Gary Cooper, Marlene Dietrich, Greta Garbo, Ernst Lubitsch and Josef von Sternberg. He also visited the studio of Walt Disney, whose animated sound films he greatly admired, and regularly played tennis with Charlie Chaplin.

Despite the numerous temptations of Hollywood's glittering social life, Eisenstein soon began work on a number of projects for his new employers. The first of these was *The Glass House*, an idea he had initially sketched out while in Berlin in 1926. Inspired in part by the utopian glass architecture of Bruno Taut, Ludwig Mies van der Rohe and Le Corbusier in Europe, as well as El Lissitzky and Ilya Golosov in the Soviet Union, *The Glass House* envisioned an American community living in a completely transparent

Sergei Eisenstein with Mickey Mouse in Hollywood, signed by Eisenstein.

building. Here, privacy was maintained not by means of obscuring walls, but by social convention, a myopic desire not to see, and thus acknowledge, the social problems and inequalities of capitalist society. Central to the plot was the gradual breakdown of this convention, ultimately resulting in a voyeuristic society gazing increasingly, with indifference, on the personal tragedies of its citizens. This concept provided ample opportunity for cinematic experimentation, not least in the potential orientation of irregular camera angles and the use of depth of field, both features that had been widely deployed in *The Old and the New*. In truth, however, *The Glass House* was never really likely to appeal to the Paramount executives. As an overt attack on passive spectatorship the project risked alienating the very movie-going audience that Hollywood was seeking. Unsurprisingly, the idea was soon abandoned.[21]

Next, Eisenstein turned his attention to a more conventional narrative. *Sutter's Gold*, based on the French author Blaise Cendrars' novel *L'Or* (1925), recounts the story of John Sutter, a nineteenth-century Swiss immigrant who settled in California and made his fortune in agriculture. As Sutter's innovation was the introduction of modern farming methods, here there was more than a faint echo of the central narrative in *The Old and the New*. In contrast to the notional successes of Soviet collectivization, however, Sutter is ruined in the great Gold Rush of 1848–9 as speculative mining lays bare his otherwise fruitful lands. *Sutter's Gold* thus offered a sobering critique of capitalist greed, resulting in the destruction of valuable natural resources as a consequence of the speculative search for a mineral of purely economic, and no practical, value. Eisenstein poured great efforts into the preparation of the script, travelling north to Sacramento and San Francisco to research his subject. He also proposed to introduce sound in an emotionally evocative, rather than a naturalistic, manner to create what he described as a terrible symphony of sounds. For example, the final death scene was to be accompanied by diabolical laughter, the sound of pickaxes shattering stones, the creak of wagon wheels crossing the Great Plains and the roaring of a crowd, all evoking the major moments in Sutter's life.[22] In the end, Paramount rejected the script on the grounds that the project would prove too expensive. It seems far more likely, however, that they feared the political backlash that might result from a movie that could so easily be interpreted as anti-capitalist propaganda.

Having rejected *Sutter's Gold*, Paramount proposed that Eisenstein prepare a scenario based on Theodore Dreiser's novel *An American Tragedy* (1925).[23] Drawing heavily on Dreiser's text, Eisenstein produced a script which revolved around the character of Clyde Griffiths, a young man torn between two women of very different social origins. Initially Griffiths falls for factory worker Roberta, pledging his future to her after she becomes pregnant. Soon, however, he meets rich socialite Sondra, and is tempted by the prospect of improving his economic circumstances through marriage. Unfortunately, Roberta now stands in the way. Griffiths decides to resolve his dilemma by murdering her, taking her out in a boat and throwing her into the water to drown. Thus, he chooses social advancement over moral duty. Yet at the crucial moment he hesitates, unable to perpetrate his proposed crime. At this stage, fate intervenes. The boat is accidentally overturned, and Griffiths and Roberta are both thrown into the water. Unable to swim, Roberta drowns, thus bringing about the outcome initially planned, despite Griffiths's change of heart. In an ironic narrative twist, he is then accused of the murder he originally intended but never executed, tried in a court of law, found guilty and sent to the electric chair.

While *An American Tragedy* has many of the attributes of a conventional Hollywood melodrama – including a love triangle, a tragic accident, a tense court case and the final death of the hero – Dreiser's novel was complex in its handling of the central character, presenting Griffiths as a victim more than a villain. For Dreiser, the true cause of the tragedy was the social injustice that led to the hero's original fateful decision and his ultimate execution. Eisenstein specifically picked up on this and, rather than focus on the more conventional aspects of the story, proposed a complex psychological analysis constructed around a Joycean inner monologue in which Griffiths's own Hamlet-like doubt was articulated through a kaleidoscope of images and sounds. Even as the Paramount executives were pondering the possibilities of producing such a movie, however, a new wave of anti-Bolshevik sentiment swept through Hollywood. In early October, the staunch anti-Communist Congressman Hamilton Fish launched an investigation into so-called Communist activities in Hollywood and specifically targeted Eisenstein. Pressure soon mounted on Paramount to justify their support for the Soviet director. No doubt fearing greater repercussions, the executives cracked and called him into the studio. He was informed that his screenplay for *An American Tragedy*, though of excellent quality, had been rejected, and, as a consequence, his contract was terminated.

It remains unclear precisely why Eisenstein's Hollywood adventure ended in such failure. Certainly his unwillingness to compromise with Hollywood's conventions and expectations made the studio executives more than a little nervous and thus reluctant to give him their full backing. In the end, however, it was probably the sheer weight of bad publicity generated by the anti-Bolshevik, anti-Eisenstein campaign that led to Paramount's decision. It was now six months since he had arrived in Hollywood and over a year since he had left the Soviet Union. Thus far he had failed to produce a single feature-length movie.

Following the termination of the Hollywood contract, Eisenstein and his colleagues began to make preparations for their return to the Soviet Union. Paramount had even agreed to pay for three single tickets to Moscow. Eisenstein, however, remained convinced that he could complete a movie in the West. Shortly before the scheduled departure date, he was introduced to the director Robert Flaherty, best known for his ethnographic/documentary films recording the life of remote communities in northern Canada (*Nanook of the North*, 1922) and the Pacific islands (*Moana*, 1926). Flaherty, who had established a reputation as something of a maverick, was all too familiar with the vagaries of the Hollywood studio system and advised Eisenstein to consider making an independent film. He even proposed a subject: Mexico. Eisenstein instantly recognized that there might be distinct political advantages in tackling such a subject. After all, the Soviet authorities were fascinated by Mexico, recognizing it as a nation that shared certain historical parallels with Russia. In 1910, for example, Mexico had staged its own revolution, nine years later establishing a Communist Party. In 1924, it also became the first New World nation to forge official diplomatic links with the Soviet Union. Recent events had also brought Mexico into the consciousness of the wider Soviet public. In 1925, Vladimir Mayakovsky had made a much publicized visit to Mexico City, on his return recounting his experiences in articles in *Krasnaya Nov.* He had even published a poem entitled 'Mexika'.[24] The following year, Diego Rivera, whose work Mayakovsky had praised, had travelled to Moscow, where he had worked on several mural commissions as well as spending time with Eisenstein. All this was likely to enhance the credibility of Eisenstein's proposed Mexican project in the eyes of the Soviet leadership, whose permission he required if he wished to extend his leave of absence.

With his usual passion for research, Eisenstein now began reading everything he could about Mexico, including John Reed's *Insurgent Mexico*, an account of the Mexican Revolution written in 1914, and Anita Brenner's recently published *Idols Behind Altars*.[25] At this stage he planned to make a vast panoramic film, recounting the entire history of the nation. His first major obstacle was to secure financing. Initially, he turned to his good friend Chaplin, who approved of his plans but failed to offer financial support. He did, however, suggest that Eisenstein approach Upton Sinclair, the left-wing political activist and novelist whose works had proved highly successful in the Soviet Union. Sinclair was instantly sympathetic to Eisenstein's plight and, despite limited experience in film production, both he and his wife Mary Craig Sinclair agreed to back the project. Within a matter of weeks they had set up a company, the Mexican Film Trust, and signed a contract with Eisenstein. It was agreed that he would to deliver a movie, provisionally entitled *Mexican Picture* (later to become *Que Viva Mexico!*) in three or four months, to a budget of $25,000. As things turned out, both time and money were woefully underestimated.[26]

In December 1930, Eisenstein, Alexandrov and Tisse set off for Mexico, accompanied by Mary Craig Sinclair's brother, Hunter Kimbrough, acting in the capacity of project manager. The timing of the trip once more turned out to be less than propitious. In March 1929, amid fears of an upsurge in political activism, the Mexican government had officially declared the Communist Party illegal, resulting in a cooling of Soviet–Mexican relations. The situation had worsened when a decree was issued banning all known Communists from entering the country. Eisenstein's arrival just a few months later inevitably generated considerable controversy. To make matters worse, Pease, still espousing his virulent anti-Bolshevik views, reportedly sent a telegram to the Mexican government denouncing Eisenstein as a Communist spy. Thus it was hardly surprising when, within a fortnight of their arrival, Eisenstein and his colleagues were taken into police custody for questioning. The storm abated, however, when Mary Craig Sinclair orchestrated an official campaign of protest which included telegrams from Albert Einstein, George Bernard Shaw, Fairbanks, Chaplin and two US senators. Eisenstein and his colleagues were released and declared honorary guests of the Mexican government. The project, however, had got off to a far from auspicious start.

Eisenstein soon began filming, shooting scenes of a fiesta and a bullfight in Guadalupe and Puebla. However, the overall shape of the film was as yet far from determined. Following Flaherty's practices, Eisenstein wanted to immerse himself in the land and get a feel for its people and culture before committing himself to any definite plans; here Diego Rivera proved an invaluable guide. In Mexico City, he introduced Eisenstein to the vibrant artistic community, including his young wife, the painter Frida Kahlo, and the muralists Jean Charlot and Roberto Montenegro, who later produced strikingly disparate portraits of Eisenstein. Charlot's small oil sketch (1932), represents Eisenstein as a modern intellectual, seen in profile with his brow furrowed and staring into the distance. Montenegro produced a far more ambiguous portrait, representing Eisenstein as a Spanish conquistador in a mural at the Mexico City Pedagogical Institute (1930–31).[27]

In early January 1931 the crew travelled south to Taxco, where Eisenstein met the muralist David Alfaro Siqueiros, and thence on to Acapulco. On hearing that an earthquake had struck in the region of Oaxaca, the team chartered an aeroplane and travelled south. Telegrams sent from Kimbrough to Sinclair suggest that they were hoping to sell footage of this tragedy to American news agencies to raise further cash for the project.[28] By the end of the month, the crew was setting off once more, this time travelling to Tehuantepec on the southern Pacific coast. This journey may well have been suggested by Rivera, who had first visited the region in 1922 and regarded the experience as revelatory for his work.[29] Like Rivera before him, Eisenstein was entranced by the lush, tropical landscape of this remote part of Mexico. He was also fascinated by the region's indigenous society and culture. After a brief return to Mexico City, the team relocated to the Yucatán Peninsula to film the remnants of Mayan civilization at Chichen Itza and Izamal.

By April, the proposed completion date had already passed, and Eisenstein was yet to produce a full scenario. Sinclair began to worry, but, having seen all the footage shot to date, remained confident that the film would prove a great success. A month later the team moved into a remote hacienda in Tetlapayac. This former Spanish plantation, surrounded by fields of maguey cacti, was to be their home for the next four months. Hampered by bad weather, illness and administrative hold-ups, progress was painfully slow, and Eisenstein spent much of his time producing a series of drawings inspired by Mexican culture both ancient and modern. Many of these, executed in a simple, exaggerated linear style, were of an explicitly erotic and homoerotic, and frequently violent, nature, a factor that would later generate problems for him. By September, Sinclair's patience had begun to wear thin. Concerned about the significant time overrun and rapidly dwindling funds, he made an

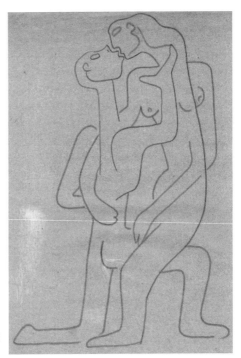

A drawing by Sergei Eisenstein.

effort to exert his authority over Eisenstein, demanding a precise schedule for completion and cuts to the budget. This, however, had little effect. In growing desperation, Sinclair even began to explore the possibility of selling the project on to a major studio, but no-one seemed willing to take further financial risks.

Throughout the autumn, Eisenstein's relationship with both Kimbrough and Sinclair deteriorated rapidly, and rumours began to spread concerning the Soviet director's motives. Sinclair suspected that he was deliberately delaying the project in order to secure more money or in the vain hope that Paramount would rehire the Soviet team. Sinclair also feared, somewhat erroneously, that Eisenstein was shooting vast quantities of footage in order make several movies, all at Sinclair's expense.[30] In the end, however, this turned out to be the least of Eisenstein's worries. During the late summer of 1931, Boris Shumyatsky, the head of Soyuzkino, wrote to him to demand his return to the Soviet Union. Shumyatsky had little time or patience for Eisenstein's international projects, believing his talents would be better deployed serving the Soviet government, not least as the fifteenth anniversary of the October Revolution was a little over a year away.[31] Ill-advisedly, Eisenstein ignored Shumyatsky's request and continued his work on *Que Viva Mexico!* This was a high-risk strategy, as Eisenstein was doubtless aware that, since the late 1920s, a number of key figures had illegally fled the Soviet Union. This had led in 1929 to an official decree stating that 'The refusal of a citizen of the Soviet Union . . . to return to the USSR upon the suggestion of an organ of state authority will be considered desertion . . . and will qualify as treason.'[32] By November, the gravity of Eisenstein's decision became all too evident when Stalin sent a telegram to Sinclair declaring that Eisenstein had now lost the confidence of his comrades in the Soviet Union. He was considered a deserter.[33] At this point, Eisenstein's world began to implode. By the beginning of 1932, Sinclair's patience finally reached its limit and he withdrew all funding. At the same time, the Soviet authorities stated that Eisenstein's residence permit was no longer valid and demanded his immediate return. The Mexican adventure had come to an ignominious end.

After a significant delay at the border, generated in part by the discovery of Eisenstein's homoerotic drawings, the team was finally allowed to re-enter the United States in mid-March, but was instructed to travel straight to New York and thence to leave the country as soon as possible. Although Eisenstein had not completed his planned shooting schedule, he still hoped to salvage something from the project and made an agreement with Sinclair that both the editing and the soundtrack would be completed back in Moscow. Thus in mid-April 1932, Eisenstein finally departed from American shores with assurances from Sinclair that the footage would be forwarded on the very next ship. Sinclair, however, no doubt fearing further delays and demands upon his purse, reneged on the deal, choosing instead to cut his losses and sell off parts of the film for other projects. Eisenstein was never to see the footage again.

In March 1933, a version of the film was released in the United States under the title *Thunder Over Mexico*. The following year, more of Eisenstein's footage turned up in *Death Day*. Both these movies, edited by Hollywood producer Sol Lesser, were greeted by a storm of protest in the American press, with Sinclair variously accused of philistinism and sabotage.

Several subsequent attempts were also made to edit the material. In 1939, Eisenstein's friend, later his biographer, Marie Seton, negotiated the right to make a new version of the film, released in 1940 under the title *Time in the Sun*, while parts of the footage also turned up in a series of educational films under the title *Mexican Symphony* (1941). In the 1950s, the film historian Jay Leyda put together parts of the footage that had been stored at the Museum of Modern Art in New York to produce what he referred to as 'study films', an attempt to allow access to the possibilities of the project rather than to replicate what might have been.

The most important of these subsequent attempts to complete the film came in the late 1970s, nearly a decade after Sinclair's death. After a campaign launched twenty years earlier, the footage was finally sent to the Soviet Union, where it was edited by the now septuagenarian Alexandrov. Thus, in 1979, over a half a century after the original material had been shot, a new version of *Que Viva Mexico!* was officially premiered at the Moscow Film Festival. Alexandrov's connection with the original project certainly suggested a high degree of authenticity for this production. The outcome, however, can at best be regarded as a generalized notion of what Eisenstein may have intended.[34]

Inevitably, all of these later versions of *Que Viva Mexico!* need to be treated with circumspection, not least as Eisenstein played no part in either the editing or sound production. Further, while some of them rely heavily on his published scenario, it is worth noting that this was probably written as much to appease Sinclair and the Mexican censors as to guide production.[35] Indeed, Eisenstein was renowned for his tendency to use scenarios as little more than rough guides during the shooting process. Given these limitations, any subsequent analysis of *Que Viva Mexico!* is necessarily contingent upon end products that are, at best, speculative. Nonetheless, it is possible to draw some tentative conclusions.

In essence, *Que Viva Mexico!* set out to offer a historical account of the social, economic and political development of Mexico from the earliest civilizations to contemporary times. This was structured around six separate episodes representing a series of teleological steps on the pathway to the revolution of 1910 and concluding with the continuing struggles of the post-revolutionary era.

The first episode acts as a prologue. Shot in Yucatán, it features both distant and close-up shots of Mayan temples and monumental statues of deities, thus establishing Mexico as a land of ancient

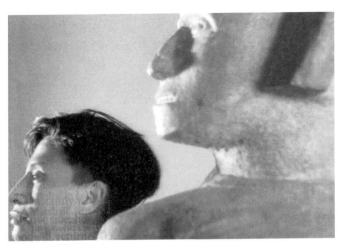

'Monuments and Men', *Que Viva Mexico!*, 1930–32.

cultures. Eisenstein notably introduces contemporary Mexicans, yet presents them as static figures posed in such a manner as to resemble the monuments that form their cultural legacy. To emphasize further the notion of Mexico as a land of the dead, the camera focuses on a funeral procession wending its way through a field of cacti. As the procession comes to rest, the faces of the mourners frame the coffin, their eyes closed much like those of the deceased. Described by Eisenstein as the 'Stones – Gods – Men' sequence, the emphasis here is on monumentality and stasis, suggesting that the entire landscape and its inhabitants have been petrified, frozen in time.

The second episode titled 'Sandunga', similarly represents the period before the Spanish Conquest. Here, however, the bleak and desolate landscape of the prologue makes way for the lush, tropical forests of Tehuantepec, presented as an idyllic paradise inhabited by semi-naked young men and women. Ancient Mexico is presented as a land of simplicity, social harmony and eternal leisure. In both the prologue and 'Sandunga', Eisenstein represents early

Mexico as an idealized world. Adopting a dialectical approach to history, the next sequence, 'Fiesta', is presented as an antithesis, marking a dramatic shift in mood and focusing explicitly on the destruction and devastation wrought by the arrival of the conquistadors in the early sixteenth century. On his first Sunday in Mexico City, Eisenstein spent the morning filming a festival in celebration of the Virgin of Guadalupe, whose legendary appearance in 1531 is regarded as the catalyst for the spread of Catholicism to the New World. In the afternoon, he shot a bullfight, or *corrida*, at the Plaza de Toros. Eisenstein later commented on the strange congruence between the ceremonies of the church and those of the *corrida*: 'It was Mexico itself mixing into one Sunday festive element. Christ's blood of the matins in the cathedral with streams of bull's blood at the afternoon *corrida* in the city arena.'[36] In 'Fiesta' he sought to juxtapose these religious and secular ceremonies, both imposed upon the indigenous population by the Spanish conquest. Here, the suffering of the bull is equated with that of Christian penitents, enticed to crawl on their knees or bear crosses made from cacti in imitation of Christ's own suffering. By extension, this suffering also represents the oppression of the indigenous population at the hands of the colonial invaders.

The fourth episode, 'Maguey', is set during the dictatorship of Porfirio Diaz at the beginning of the twentieth century. Shot at the hacienda in Tetlapayac, 'Maguey' recounts the story of Sebastian, a native peon (roughly equivalent to a serf), who, following the rape of his fiancée Maria, takes up arms against his Spanish colonial masters. After a gun battle during which the daughter of the local landowner is killed, Sebastian and his fellow-conspirators are captured and executed in a horrific fashion, buried in the ground up to their necks and then trampled to death by horses. The brutality of this scene, reminiscent of the massacres in *Strike*, *Potemkin* and *October*, brings us closest to Eisenstein's more familiar emphasis on class conflict, exploitation and rebellion.

'Execution of the Peons', *Que Viva Mexico!*

Here, he leaves us in no doubt that it is the local workers who are the true victims in this historical drama. In the context of the recent suppression of left-wing opposition, the 'Maguey' story also implies the continuing brutality of the Mexican government.

The conflict central to both 'Fiesta' and 'Maguey' is presented as a catalyst for the revolution of 1910, which was to be recounted in the next episode, entitled 'Soldadera'. However, none of this sequence was shot before Sinclair pulled the plug on the project. As the principal revolutionary episode in the film, 'Soldadera' was nonetheless intended to provide the dialectical synthesis in Eisenstein's historical account. It recounted the story of Pancha, one of the eponymous *soldaderas*, or soldiers' wives, who accompanied their husbands to the front. Within the proposed narrative, Pancha fell pregnant and gave birth at the precise moment that her husband was killed in battle. Rather than mourn his loss, however, she immediately took up with another soldier who would care for her child, thus signifying revolutionary continuity in the context of the cycle of life and death. Later Eisenstein claimed that Pancha's acceptance of a new husband was also intended to symbolize the allegiance of the revolutionary factions of Pancho Villa and Emiliano Zapata, and thus 'the union of all the people against the forces of reaction'.[37]

The sixth and final episode in *Que Viva Mexico!*, constructed as an epilogue, brings the movie up to the present day, focusing on the Day of the Dead, when Mexicans honour the deceased, celebrating their passage into a new life. In this sequence, Eisenstein highlights the joyous, carnivalistic aspects of the festival, focusing on the paraphernalia that accompany the celebrations: toys in the shape of skeletons, sweets in the form of skulls, and the skull masks worn by the participants. With its emphasis on ceremonials surrounding death, the epilogue brings the narrative full circle, echoing the funeral scene central to the prologue and thus reconfirming Eisenstein's emphasis on the eternal cycle of life. The sequence concludes with shots of workers, peasants and children removing their masks to reveal smiling faces, an optimistic image of Mexico's future. As a final wry political comment, Eisenstein contrasts these shots with the unmasking of priests, government officials and military leaders to reveal not human visages, but real skulls, thus signifying that the period of the domination of the bourgeoisie is now over.

In adopting a dialectical approach to history, each episode within Eisenstein's account of Mexico presupposes the inevitable rise and fall of capitalism, here symbolized by the colonial occupiers. In this way, the historical account collapses the temporal stability of each of the scenes, presenting past and present simultaneously. In a typically metaphorical vein, Eisenstein associated this coexistence of past and present with the sarape, or striped blanket, traditionally worn in Mexico, in which the violently contrasting colours of the stripes represented 'the cultures in Mexico running next to each other and at the same time being centuries away'.[38] This is most evident in the prologue and 'Sandunga', both of which simultaneously represent a timeless past inhabited by contemporary

'Unveiling the Mask', *Que Viva Mexico!*

Mexicans. Indeed, Eisenstein notably described Tehuantepec, the setting for 'Sandunga', as 'a typically pre-Columbian environment, which has been preserved in the tropical provinces up to the present'.[39] This somewhat problematic collapsing of ancient and modern histories was clearly influenced by Eisenstein's interests in contemporary anthropology and ethnology, not least Lucien Lévy-Bruhl's ideas concerning so called 'primitive' mentalities.[40] However, other influences for this way of conceiving the history of Mexico lay closer to home, not least in the representations of history articulated in the work of the Mexican muralists.

Having met Rivera in Moscow, Eisenstein was certainly aware of this movement prior to his trip to Mexico. Brenner's *Idols Behind Altars* also reacquainted him with it. Nothing, however, had fully prepared him for the experience of seeing the murals at first hand. In Mexico City he visited all of the major mural sites, including the National Preparatory School (with murals by Siqueiros, Jose Clemente Orozco and Rivera); the Ministry of Education building (with its cycle of 235 frescoes produced by Rivera and his assistants between 1923 and 1928); and the National Palace (where Rivera had recently completed part of his series of frescoes based on *The History of Mexico*).[41] Echoes of these works resound throughout *Que Viva Mexico!* For example, the burial sequence in the prologue was based explicitly on Siqueiros's *Burial of a Sacrificed Worker*, part of the National Preparatory School mural produced in 1922 and also illustrated in *Idols Behind Altars*. Similarly, the visual style of 'Maguey' can be compared with Orozco's murals exploring the corruption and social injustice of the Spanish conquest, also at the National Preparatory School. Orozco's panels *The Trench* and *Revolutionary Trinity* offer a particularly striking visual counterpoint to Eisenstein's representation of the executions of Sebastian and his fellow peons, while the muralist's images of *soldaderas* may well have also influenced Eisenstein's decision to base his penultimate episode on this character. However, the artist whose work left the greatest mark on Eisenstein's conception of Mexico was, without doubt, Rivera. One might even go further and argue that *Que Viva Mexico!* can be read as a cinematic paean to the Mexican artist. Indeed, the points of comparison between *Que Viva Mexico!* and Rivera's murals at both the Ministry of Education and the National Palace are extensive. For example, both works place great emphasis on the Pre-Columbian cultural heritage.[42] Similarly, representations of the local, indigenous population dominate Rivera's murals much as they do Eisenstein's film. The use of regional diversity as a structural principle is also evident in both artists' work. For example, they include close-up details of regional flora, not least the distinctive maguey cactus. There also seems to be little doubt that Eisenstein's extensive focus on regional ceremonies and festivities, a central feature of all the completed sequences in *Que Viva Mexico!*, derives largely from Rivera's similar focus in the Court of Fiestas at the Ministry of Education building. Here, not least of all, Rivera's three panels representing the Day of the Dead were clearly an inspiration for Eisenstein's epilogue.

Nor was it just in subject matter that Eisenstein drew upon Rivera's work. As Desmond Rochfort has argued, one striking feature of the Ministry of Education murals is the regular reworking of biblical themes, in which the Mexican peasant is cast as a secular parallel to Christian martyrs.[43] Eisenstein readily adopted this strategy in *Que Viva Mexico!*, most obviously in the execution of Sebastian and his fellow peons in the 'Maguey' sequence. Even naming his hero Sebastian explicitly recalled the notion of Christian martyrdom that Eisenstein had earlier updated in *October*.

Eisenstein's decision to construct his film as a parallel to Rivera's murals made a great deal of sense. After all, his working practices as a filmmaker had many affinities with those of the Mexican muralists. Both used overtly political subject matter within explicitly public art forms, produced primarily to educate the masses. Further, mural painting and film production were essentially collective endeavours, involving teams of workers labouring together, though organized under the leadership of a single individual.[44] It could also be argued that the decorative schemes produced by Rivera and the other Mexican muralists have a distinctly cinematic quality, featuring multiple images combined – one might even say montaged – into a carefully orchestrated sequence to produce a visual and aesthetic ensemble. Further, the frequent use of text – in the form of slogans, declarations and poems – introduced to clarify the message of a mural is not entirely dissimilar to the use of inter-titles in silent cinema.[45]

Eisenstein openly acknowledged his debt to Rivera, not least his dialectical conception of Mexican history, in an outline of *Que Viva Mexico!* sent to Sinclair in October 1931:

In the production of this motion picture in which we are presently engaged it is our purpose and desire to make an artistic portrayal of the contrasting beauty of natural scenery, costumes, customs, art and human types in Mexico and to

José Guadalupe
Posada, *Skull*, print.

show the people in relation to their natural environment and
social evolution. To combine mountains, seas, deserts, ruins of
ancient civilization and the people of the past and present into a
symphonic cinema, symphonic from the standpoint of construction and arrangement, might be comparable in a sense to
the paintings by Diego Rivera in the National Palace. Like these
paintings our picture will portray the social evolution of Mexico
from ancient times to the present time when it emerges as a
modern progressive country of liberty and opportunity.[46]

However, Eisenstein was also conscious that, back in the Soviet
Union, too close an association with Rivera might prove problematic. When the Soviet director had arrived in Mexico, Rivera was
still a committed socialist. In September 1929, however, he had been
expelled from the Mexican Communist Party and was beginning to

shift his political allegiance from Stalin to the now exiled Trotsky. By 1937, albeit several years after Eisenstein's return to the Soviet Union, Rivera's support for Trotsky extended to offering the former head of the Red Army refuge at his home in Tampico. Throughout the rest of his life, Eisenstein acknowledged Rivera's role in introducing him to aspects of Mexican culture. It could certainly be argued, however, that he underplayed the extent to which Rivera's murals provided the single most important model for *Que Viva Mexico!*

Brief mention should also be made of other cultural influences that left their mark on Eisenstein's movie. For example, he was a particular admirer of the woodcuts of José Guadalupe Posada, whom he regarded as the spiritual father of Mexican modern art.[47] Posada's political illustrations and caricatures, many produced as broadsheets and in the popular left-wing press in the years immediately prior to the revolution of 1910, are relentless in their critique of the authorities, frequently highlighting the kind of brutality Eisenstein was only too willing to explore in *Que Viva Mexico!* Posada is best known, however, for his *calaveras*, satirical images of Mexico's upper classes depicted as living skeletons. While Eisenstein saw many of Posada's illustrations in Mexico, it is notable that two images illustrated in Brenner's *Idols Behind Altars* bear a remarkable similarity to scenes from his movie. The first of these features a working woman who is being punished by having a tree trunk tied across her shoulders.[48] Eisenstein's image of the Christian penitents in 'Fiesta' notably replicates this form of suffering. Even more striking, however, is Posada's image of a skeleton dressed in the uniform of a naval officer, which Eisenstein quoted directly in his Day of the Dead sequence.[49]

The influence of the photographers Edward Weston and Tina Modotti, who spent much time in Mexico during the 1920s, can also be felt in *Que Viva Mexico!*[50] Although Weston and Modotti had left the country before Eisenstein arrived, their work was familiar to

'Monuments and Men', *Que Viva Mexico!*

him, once again through reproductions in Brenner's book. Weston's stark, monumental images of Mayan pyramids and close-ups of pots, palm trunks and maguey cacti clearly left their mark on Tisse's photography, not least in his sharp focus and use of filters to heighten contrast.[51] Modotti, whose more politically oriented works appeared in the journals *Mexican Folkways* and *El Machete*, placed greater emphasis on workers and peasants, typically dressed in traditional costumes. Once again, many sequences in *Que Viva Mexico!* bear a remarkable affinity to these works both in their composition and mood. All of this suggests the extent to which Eisenstein visualized Mexico not only through his immediate experience of the nation but also through his awareness of representations in other media.

In the end, his failure to complete *Que Viva Mexico!* constituted one of the greatest disappointments of Eisenstein's career. It also ensured that his sojourn abroad was seen by many in the Soviet Union as an ignominious failure. In fact, the project might best be described as his unfinished symphony.

5

Reprieve

Eisenstein finally arrived back in Moscow in May 1932 after an absence of nearly three years. His failure to produce a single film of note during this period, added to the numerous controversies that had surrounded his trips to Paris, Hollywood and Mexico, ensured that his return was far from triumphal. Nonetheless, he remained the Soviet Union's best-known director, and a host of press photographers turned out to record the event. Even Shumyatsky made an appearance, though hardly as a member of a welcoming committee. As he stepped onto the platform at Belorusskaya station, Eisenstein must have wondered to what extent his sojourn abroad had impacted on his domestic reputation and what effect this would have on his future.

The cultural climate to which Eisenstein returned was dramatically different from that he had left in 1929. During his absence, the Soviet Union had undergone a cultural revolution as the state increasingly stamped its authority on cultural activity. In April 1932, for example, an official decree was issued banning the existence of independent groups of writers and artists. Recognizing that many of these generated little more than factional infighting, the state now aimed to draw a line under past practices and establish a unified cultural policy for the future. At the 1934 Soviet Writers' Congress this policy was unveiled as Socialist Realism, officially declared to be the only approved cultural model.

The film industry had also entered something of a crisis in

Eisenstein's absence as it witnessed a dramatic fall in production. In 1931, for example, 103 new films had been released, compared with 146 in 1930. The following year, production had fallen further to just 90 new releases, and in 1933 to a paltry 35.[1] The fact that imported films had also been banned only served to exacerbate the sense of crisis. The Soviet Union's ambition to produce its own film stock and convert to sound certainly contributed to this decline. However, the demand that all new films conform to the tenets of Socialist Realism at a time when it was far from clear precisely what this actually would involve, also played its part. With ever more stringent censorship bodies being put in place, the maxim of the day was increasingly: if in doubt, ban it.

It was during this crisis that Eisenstein returned to work, his reputation shaken, but still reasonably intact. Initially, he was invited to produce a musical comedy, but he regarded the offer as a deliberate snub and turned it down. Alexandrov, however, accepted the commission and set up on his own, parting company with Eisenstein and Tisse. The resulting film, *The Happy Guys* (1934), turned out to be one of the most popular movies of the inter-war period. Perhaps in response to Alexandrov's departure, and in recognition of the shift in emphasis towards popular-entertain-ment movies, Eisenstein next worked on a script for a comedy of his own, titled *ммм*. The eponymous hero of the proposed movie, one Maxim Maximovich Maximov, was employed as a tour guide, showing visitors around a modern, but unnamed, city. His guests, however, were not from another city or country, but from the past, specifically sixteenth-century Muscovy. This plot provided Eisenstein with an opportunity to collapse past and present and thus highlight the incongruities of modern life. At the same time, the emphasis on the alienation of the visitor doubtless reflected his own experiences on returning from abroad while also offering a wry commentary on the alienation of the 1.5 million new inhabi-tants, mostly migrants from the countryside, who had moved to

Moscow during the first Five-Year Plan.[2] Eisenstein was handsomely paid for the script, but *MMM* never reached production.[3]

His next project, a cinematic history of the city of Moscow, was as ambitious in scope as *Que Viva Mexico!* As Eisenstein worked on the scenario, huge swathes of the city were being demolished as part of the plan for its reconstruction. Typically, Eisenstein's proposal was far from being a straightforward historical account. Rather, he structured the project around the four elements of earth, air, fire and water, while also exploring the possibility of deploying a Joycean inner monologue as a central aspect of the screenplay. Although *Moscow* was officially contracted to Soyuzkino, the film was never made.

Undaunted by his failure to get these projects onto the screen, Eisenstein returned to an idea he had first conceived in Hollywood two years earlier. *The Black Consul,* an account of the Haitian slave rebellion of the 1790s, seemed at first glance to be an appropriate subject for official approval, although the fact that the main revolutionary leaders, Henri Christophe and François-Dominique Toussaint-L'Ouverture, had both ended up as dictators perhaps put something of a risky slant on the tale. As with *MMM* and *Moscow*, initial support for the project was strong, and Eisenstein even invited the American singer, actor, Civil Rights activist and supporter of the Soviet Union, Paul Robeson, to Moscow to discuss the project. When Robeson arrived in December 1934 he received a warm welcome. Once again, however, Eisenstein's proposal fell on stony ground.

Seemingly unable to get a film project beyond the planning stage, Eisenstein immersed himself in research and spent much of 1933 and '34 working on a proposed book to be titled *Fundamental Problem*. At the same time he was invited to teach at GIK (State Institute of Cinematography), where he had briefly taught in 1928. It was also towards the end of this period, in October 1934, that he entered into a marriage of convenience with Pera Atasheva. As the relationship was, by all accounts, purely platonic, it can only be conjectured that Eisenstein was here attempting to protect himself against accusations of homosexuality, not least in the wake of the introduction of legislation earlier that year making homosexuality an offence punishable by up to five years' imprisonment. The public scandal surrounding the homoerotic drawings found in his suitcase at the Mexican border three years earlier might have made him nervous. Thus, by the end of 1934, Eisenstein's earlier reputation as a young, dynamic, innovative and revolutionary practitioner had been largely transformed. He was now increasingly regarded as an old, ascetic, erudite and slightly eccentric theoretician who had largely divorced himself from actual filmmaking.

The problematic nature of this reputation was to be made all too evident at a major event held at the Bolshoi Theatre in January 1935. The All-Union Creative Conference of Workers in Soviet Cinema, staged in honour of the fifteenth anniversary of the nationalization of the film industry, was, in effect, the cinematic equivalent of the Soviet Writers' Congress, an attempt to draw a line under past achievements and determine an officially sanctioned way forward for the industry. In particular the conference highlighted the impor-tance of clear narrative structure (the legibility argument that been first been raised in 1928), the promotion of positive heroes, and the importance of cinema in both entertaining and educating the younger generation. The recently released Civil War drama *Chapayev* was highlighted as a prototype for future productions.[4] Invited to address the audience, Eisenstein gave a long speech in which, somewhat controversially, he outlined his latest theoretical interests, including his recent ideas on the concept of inner monologue. He also reiterated his belief in the importance of montage, at a time when the word had become virtually synonymous with the formalism that was anathema to contemporary critics.

Perhaps as an inevitable consequence of this recalcitrance, Eisenstein came in for heavy criticism. As Richard Taylor has argued, however, this criticism needs to be seen in context.[5] For example, the general tone of the conference was to highlight recent shortcomings in the industry, and in this regard Eisenstein was far from alone in being identified. Further, the main criticism levelled against him was that he had spent too much time conducting theoretical research without putting any of this into practice. Eisenstein was thus called upon to forsake his theoretical meanderings and apply himself to practical endeavours. By early 1935 it was clear that his star had somewhat waned in the eyes of the Soviet authorities, yet he was far from being ostracized. For example, following the conference he was given the official title 'Honoured Artist of the Soviet Union' (although higher honours had been bestowed on most of his colleagues and contemporaries).[6] He had also recently been assigned a large flat in the House of Film Workers near the Potylikha studios on the outskirts of Moscow, a rare honour. Immediately after the conference, Eisenstein announced that he would soon begin work on a new project, a film entitled *Bezhin Meadow*. This, he hoped, would both re-establish his flagging reputation and prove his political loyalties. As things turned out, it was to be yet another false dawn.

The screenplay for *Bezhin Meadow*, written by Alexander Rzheshevsky, drew both its title and its inspiration from a short story by the nineteenth-century novelist Ivan Turgenev. Rzheshevsky, however, transported this tale to the present day and built his narrative around a contemporary figure, a young pioneer clearly based on the real-life Soviet child-hero Pavlik Morozov. In 1932, the body of the teenage Pavlik had been found in the woods surrounding the remote village of Gerasimovka. He had been murdered by his relatives in revenge, as he had denounced his own father to the authorities. As Catriona Kelly has pointed out, Pavlik's murder was neither a unique occurrence in the early Soviet period nor one that immediately attracted wide publicity.[7] Within a couple of years, however, a veritable cult of the child-martyr had grown up, much promoted by the writer Maxim Gorky. The elevation of Pavlik to cult status notably coincided with a wider campaign to promote the childhood theme in novels and plays, painting and sculpture, and music and film. The representation of children as symbols of the bright future of the Soviet nation became increasingly associated with officially sanctioned Socialist Realism.

The *Bezhin Meadow* commission thus offered Eisenstein an ideal opportunity to redeem himself in the eyes of the authorities. Firstly, the project explored the same conflict between modernity and tradition in the countryside that had shaped the heavily criticized *The Old and the New*, thus giving him a chance to prove, once and for all, that he had learned from his notional mistakes. Secondly, the focus on an individual hero, the young Pavlik (renamed Stepok in Rzheshevsky's screenplay), rather than the masses, suggested that Eisenstein might now prove his credentials as a Socialist Realist filmmaker. As Shumyatsky later argued, the *Bezhin Meadow* project provided Eisenstein with an opportunity 'to face up to the new requirements that had in the main emerged in the years of his long creative silence'.[8] Perhaps most important of all, however, was the main ideological message of the movie: the promotion of unflinching loyalty to the state. With the worst excesses of Stalin's purges now beginning to take hold, Eisenstein was doubtless keen to prove his own commitment.

As if to confirm his change of direction, Eisenstein broke with his previous practices by recruiting professional actors to play key roles, doubtless a response to criticism of his earlier emphasis on types, rather than individuals, as the central protagonists in his movies. The part of Stepok, however, was reserved for an unknown peasant boy by the name of Vitya Kartashov, selected from a group of over 2,000 children. In May, once the script had been cleared by the censors, filming began in earnest. Among the crew were Pera Atasheva, taking over Alexandrov's role as director's assistant, and four of Eisenstein's students from GIK including the American, Jay

Leyda, recruited as production historian and stills photographer.[9] Despite Eisenstein's initial assurances to the contrary, once on the set, he soon reverted to his old improvisatory practices. As Leyda pointed out, 'I have seen more than one filming day pass without Eisenstein referring once to the script – so reliant is he upon the firm mental images he keeps with him. He says that all plans are to prepare you for new ideas that the day's work brings.'[10] Eisenstein also began to introduce the very poetic-symbolic strategies for which he had been so severely criticized. To take one example, he began filming by shooting close-ups of blossoming trees in an orchard in Kolomenskoye, near Moscow. These shots, reminiscent of the closing sequence of *Romance sentimentale*, were to form a prologue described by Leyda as 'an evocation of Turgenev':

> These first shots were taken with an understanding of Turgenev's place in and contribution to the history of literature and art. In the wake of romanticism, Turgenev was attracted by the impressionists, who were in turn attracted by the Japanese printmakers; Turgenev's introduction of impressionism into literature was the key the episode needed.[11]

While this sequence may well have been precisely what Eisenstein required, it was hardly in keeping with the ideological message of the proposed movie. Nor, it might be added, were his ideas for audio-visual montage. In one scene, for example, he proposed that angry peasant voices be transformed into wailing sirens, thus recalling the experimental sound montage he had considered for *Sutter's Gold*. Throughout the film he introduced direct quotations from his previous work. For example, in a scene featuring the dismantling of a church, several peasants are shown curiously examining icons, vestments and other religious paraphernalia in a sequence that directly parallels scenes from *October*. To reinforce this parallel, shots of a young boy donning a crown far too large for his head clearly echo the young child occupying the Tsar's throne towards the end of the earlier film. The symbolic use of dark and light, including the use of a halo-like illumination behind the head of the young Stepok, also recalls both *October* and *The Old and the New*, while the deployment of an exaggerated depth of field reflects Eisenstein's, and Tisse's, continued interest in the effect of wide-angle lenses. Similarly, the emphasis on a funeral procession towards the beginning of *Bezhin Meadow* recalls the prologue to *Que Viva Mexico!*, while the inclusion of a young child staring with amusement at a representation of a skull inevitably references the Day of the Dead sequence. Even the firefighting sequence carries reminiscences of *Strike*. As shooting advanced on *Bezhin Meadow*, it became increasingly clear that Eisenstein was, in fact, willing to make relatively few concessions to the demands of Socialist Realism.

In early 1936, the cultural climate took another turn for the worse as the Soviet authorities launched a widespread campaign against formalism in the arts. In January *Pravda* published the first of several attacks against the composer Dmitry Shostakovich. Criticisms of other notable cultural figures, including the painter Pavel Filonov and the writer Mikhail Bulgakov, soon followed. Most concerning of all for Eisenstein, however, was the attack directed against his old mentor, Vsevolod Meyerkhold. As filming of *Bezhin Meadow* neared completion, Eisenstein showed the footage to Shumyatsky, who was far from pleased. Shumyatsky claimed that Eisenstein had failed adequately to represent the class struggle in the countryside, had dwelt too much on the individual-istic relationship between father and son, and had indulged exces-sively in biblical and mythological references.[12] Though clearly downhearted, Eisenstein took much of this criticism on the chin. In response he recruited a new scriptwriter, Isaak Babel, replaced some of the actors and toned down the more experimental elements of the production. Despite interruptions caused by ill health, he continued to work on *Bezhin Meadow* until March 1937, when production was suddenly called to a halt by official decree. Two days later, Shumyatsky published an article in *Pravda* condemning Eisenstein for treating his material 'subjectively and arbitrarily'.[13] Rather than depicting the 'struggle of the remnants of class-hostile elements against the creation of a new life', Eisenstein was presenting 'a veritable bacchanalia of destruction', in which 'collective farm workers are portrayed as vandals'.[14] The film, Shumyatsky declared, was 'anti-artistic and politically quite unsound'.[15] *Bezhin Meadow* was subsequently banned.

Once more, Eisenstein had spent the best part of two years working on a project only to be prevented from completing it. Unlike *Que Viva Mexico!*, however, the *Bezhin Meadow* footage was never to see the light of day as the only copy was reportedly destroyed when a German bomb hit the Mosfilm studio vaults during the Second World War. Indeed the movie is now known only through a 30-minute reconstruction put together in 1967 by Sergei Yutkevich and Naum Kleiman based on stills found in Eisenstein's archive after his death. While the Yutkevich/Kleiman production is invaluable in providing the only visual access to *Bezhin Meadow*, it inevitably constitutes, at best, a highly limited basis for any analysis or interpretation of Eisenstein's work.

In the aftermath of Shumyatsky's virulent attack on *Bezhin Meadow*, Eisenstein's reputation in the Soviet Union sunk to a new low. In February, for example, shortly before the axe finally fell, he was still eagerly contemplating a new production based on the Spanish Civil War and had gone as far as contacting Robeson to invite him to play the part of a Moroccan soldier. This, along with several other proposals, was soon abandoned. More worrying, however, was the fact that Shumyatsky's criticisms extended beyond production values, declaring Eisenstein personally responsible for the waste of 2,000,000 roubles and claiming that he had deliberately deceived both the film industry and the public. In the context of increasing arrests on the grounds of supposed sabotage, these were serious charges indeed. Within days, a conference was organized to address the situation, and pressure was put on Eisenstein to recant publicly. Accordingly, on 17 April 1937, he published an article in *Sovetskoe Iskusstvo* entitled 'The Mistakes of *Bezhin Meadow*'. Here he accepted all the criticisms that had been levelled against him, acknowledging that he had allowed himself to become too alienated from life.[16]

Eisenstein, at this point, must have feared not just for his career, but for his very existence. While he had been working on *Bezhin Meadow*, the first Moscow show trial had taken place, resulting in the execution of sixteen so-called enemies of the state, including the former members of the Politburo Grigory Zinoviev and Lev Kamenev. Over the following months, yet more former Bolsheviks were arrested and condemned to death. Although the cultural community was still relatively safe from arrest at this time, the coming years would witness the incarceration and execution of the writers Babel and Tretyakov, as well as Meyerkhold, all of whom had worked closely with Eisenstein. In January 1938, the film industry itself was targeted, and Shumyatsky, along with other major studio directors, was arrested. Six months later, when Shumyatsky was executed, Eisenstein must have feared that all this was a little too close for comfort.

In the immediate aftermath of the *Bezhin Meadow* episode, Eisenstein's health took a turn for the worse, and in May he left for a sanatorium in the Caucasus to recuperate from heart problems. Immediately before his departure, however, he grabbed the bull by the horns and sent a letter directly to Stalin pleading for the opportunity to make another film. Although raising his head above the parapet at this precise moment was doubtless a risky strategy, it appears to have paid off. While it remains unclear whether or not Stalin personally intervened, Eisenstein was offered one more opportunity to redeem himself. He was commissioned to work on a film radically different to any of his previous productions, a historical epic recounting the exploits of the thirteenth-century prince, saint and defender of Russian lands Alexander Nevsky.

Given the precariousness of his circumstances, Eisenstein was only too willing to accept this new commission, despite the fact that there were strings attached. For example, to ensure that he did not stray again, he was assigned a co-director, Dmitry Vasiliev, and his authority over casting was limited. Most of the cast now came from stage and screen backgrounds with the lead reserved for Nikolai Cherkasov, a popular star who had recently won great acclaim for playing the part of Gorky in Mikhail Romm's movie *Lenin in 1918*. The original screenplay was also co-written with Pyotr Pavlenko, a former student of Eisenstein's who was known as a staunch defender of Stalin with possible close connections to the secret police.[17] Yet Eisenstein was to get his own way regarding one key aspect of the film. The composer Sergei Prokofiev was commissioned to write the musical score.

Towards the end of 1937, the original screenplay, at this stage entitled *Rus*, was submitted to the censors. Following its publication in the journal *Znamya*, a debate ensued resulting in Eisenstein and Pavlenko being criticized for a lack of historical veracity. The main bone of contention was the proposed conclusion of the film, showing the death of Nevsky and bringing the narrative forward by over a century to highlight his victory as a precursor of Dmitry Donskoy's victory over the Tatars at Kulikova Fields in 1380.[18] While these criticisms may well have played their part, Eisenstein later offered a more intriguing explanation for the eventual decision to end the narrative immediately after the victorious battle on the ice. A black line, he claimed, was drawn across the script at the point before Nevsky's death and the words appended, 'The screenplay ends here . . . a Prince as good as that cannot die.'[19] The clear implications of this claim were that Stalin himself had intervened, though this is far from proven.[20]

Over the next few months, Eisenstein and Pavlenko reworked the screenplay and, in the process, proposed several alternative titles, including *Lord Novgorod* and *The Battle on the Ice*. Eventually the film was named in honour of its hero. In the spring, Eisenstein travelled to Novgorod to explore the possibility of shooting in situ, but the relatively poor condition of the historical buildings there persuaded him to produce the entire film in the Mosfilm studios. Models of Novgorod's cathedrals were thus built and artificial ice and snow created for the battle sequences, shot at the height of summer. Progress was rapid, and the film was completed in just five months and ahead of schedule. In early November, it was shown to Stalin for approval. Unfortunately, at this precise time Eisenstein was still editing one of the reels, which was thus left out of the preview. As this was not noticed during the screening, and as Stalin approved the film in the form in which he saw it, the missing reel was omitted from the released version despite Eisenstein's requests to the contrary. On 23 November 1938 *Alexander Nevsky* was premiered in Moscow in Stalin's presence. The Soviet leader, delighted with the film, reportedly approached Eisenstein at the end of the evening and shook him by the hand, declaring, 'You are a good Bolshevik after all!'[21] Nor was Stalin alone in praising *Alexander Nevsky*. On its public release it became a box-office smash and, following foreign distribution, was widely praised throughout Europe and the United States. In February 1939 Eisenstein was officially awarded the Order of Lenin and, one month later, an honorary doctorate from VGIK (All Union State Cinema Institute). He was, once more, headline news.

Though frequently criticized for its lack of historical exactitude, *Alexander Nevsky* was intended to be less a history lesson than a parable on the contemporary political situation. Like *Bezhin Meadow*, it sought specifically to highlight the treachery of those opposing Soviet authority. Now, however, the emphasis was less on the enemy within than on the threats posed by the outside world.

In the context of the late 1930s, this explicitly meant the rise of National Socialism in Germany. Throughout the decade, the Soviet Union had become increasingly concerned about the vulnerability of its borderlands, thus altering fundamentally the trajectory of the early Bolshevik aspiration of world revolution towards defence of national territory. Nowhere was this shift in policy more concretely manifested than on the western border. There the Soviet Union constructed an extensive system of bunkers, hidden ditches and anti-tank traps, running from Pskov in the north-west to the Black Sea coast – a 1,500-kilometre defensive barrier dubbed the Stalin Line. This concern for border defence also left its mark on wider cultural activities as the border guard became a stock character celebrated in literature, cinema and the visual arts.[22]

This concern for the potential vulnerability of the Soviet borderlands permeates virtually every scene in *Alexander Nevsky*. For example, in the opening sequence the lands of Rus are threatened not by one, but by two enemies, the Mongols and the Teutonic Knights. While some seek revenge against recent defeats at the hands of the Mongol horde, Prince Alexander Nevsky turns his attention to the more pressing danger from the west. Here, the clear message to contemporary audiences was that Nazi Germany posed a more immediate danger than the Japanese Empire, at this time fighting in Manchuria. In Nevsky's time, however, Rus had not been a united nation, but a conglomeration of city-states. Fearing imminent invasion, the peasant masses in the film – rather than the feudal lords, who advocate appeasing the enemy – call upon Nevsky to unite the Russian lands, thus breaking down the borders that divide these regions and strengthening national identity.

Throughout *Alexander Nevsky*, Eisenstein uses visual devices to signify the importance of the border. For example, the movie opens with expansive shots of the boundless lands of ancient Rus upon which the bones of the victims of the recent conflict with the Mongol horde still lie bleached by sun and wind. Next the camera

'Vigilance', *Alexander Nevsky*, 1938.

pans out to the lands beyond Lake Pleshcheyevo, predicting the
importance that lakes, as geopolitical boundaries, will play later in
the film. The first notable figure to appear is a peasant standing by a
wooden hut high above the lake and surveying his surroundings – a
direct reference to the importance of border vigilance. At this point,
the camera cuts to a shot of local fishermen holding nets in a line.
While this clearly signifies peaceful activity, the fishermen notably
carry the nets across the foreground to form a barrier, albeit a
vulnerable one, dividing the viewer from the distant horizon. To
reinforce the importance of border defence, they sing a doleful
melody recounting Nevsky's earlier victory against the Swedes.

In a later scene the fishing net is notably reintroduced, deployed
once more as a signifier for boundaries or borders. Set in Nevsky's
hut in Pereslavl, this scene highlights two young fishermen repair-
ing a net and complaining to each other about the menial nature of

'Fishermen with Nets', *Alexander Nevsky*.

their labour at a time when they believe they should be fighting instead. Their comments draw Nevsky's attention and suggest to him the need to change his military tactics from defence to attack, a shift articulated by a gesture in which he contemplates the net itself before tearing it. Yet this net signifies not only the boundary between Nevsky and the Teutonic Knights but also the barriers that need to be broken down between the fractious city-states of ancient Rus itself. Thus, when a tribune arrives from Novgorod to ask for Nevsky's help to defend that threatened city, the net is carefully removed to allow the visiting dignitaries access to him and, thus, to Pereslavl. Here the internal border is dismantled to facilitate the unification of Rus and strengthen the forces that will eventually bring about the capitulation of the invaders.

The most significant engagement with the border, however, comes in the most famous scene from the film, the battle on the ice. Shortly before the battle, Nevsky declares that the fighting must take place there, resisting the pleas of his soldiers to fight on familiar Russian soil where 'every stone is a friend, every gully a sister'. This, on the one hand, is declared as necessary to prevent the enemy from setting a single foot on Russian soil, a somewhat inconsistent argument as the film has already shown the fall of Pskov. However, it is also in recognition of the facts that the ice is thin at this time of year and that the Germans, with their heavier armour, will be vulnerable should it break up. As the battle unfolds, Nevsky's prediction proves sound, and, in a harrowing scene probably inspired by Lillian Gish's famous scene in Griffith's *Way Down East*, the Teutonic Knights are cruelly drowned in the freezing waters, literally on the very borders of ancient Rus.

Nevsky's ultimate triumph in the battle on the ice is thus recorded as a victory of national unification over regionalism and an affirmation of border integrity. Yet it is also a victory for heroic

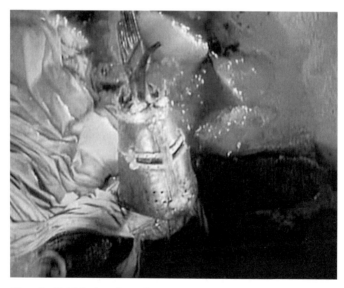

'Drowning Knight', *Alexander Nevsky*.

'Nevsky as Warrior', *Alexander Nevsky*.

individualism, and the entire plot notably revolves around the film's eponymous hero, clearly intended to be a thinly veiled representation of Stalin. What is perhaps of more interest, however, is the specific mode of representation deployed. Certainly Nevsky is presented in hagiographic mode as a two-dimensional, archetypal hero. He is unflinchingly brave, unswervingly confident, a great military strategist and in every way a natural leader of men. His presence, always assured, commands the respect of the masses, while his speech, though simple and accessible, is always inspiring. Notably, Eisenstein's depiction of him conforms to contemporary representations of Stalin, where the leader is typically represented as static, quietly thoughtful and modestly dressed, a topos in marked contrast to the more dynamic representations of Lenin. To emphasize these qualities, Eisenstein frequently shot Nevsky from a low angle, often raised on a plinth-like platform and posed against a background of buildings or sky, thus lending his hero a distinctly monumental, even statuesque, quality. Despite the urgency of the narrative, Nevsky is rarely seen in action, and when he appears among the masses, his dominant presence leaves no doubt as to his identity as first among equals.

Yet perhaps the most striking aspect of Eisenstein's presentation of Nevsky is the clear allusion to religiosity. In their research, Pavlenko and Eisenstein drew heavily upon ancient Russian chronicles which recount Nevsky's triumph as a holy victory of the Orthodox Church. Indeed Nevsky was later elevated to sainthood for his heroic deeds. Given the atheistic ideology of the Soviet state, Eisenstein inevitably underplayed associations between Nevsky and the Church, presenting him ostensibly as a secular leader. Yet undercurrents of Christian symbolism permeate the movie. For example, when Nevsky first appears he is represented as a humble fisherman, but is soon called upon by the masses to lead them to salvation. His entry into Novgorod at the beginning of the film, and into Pskov towards the conclusion, both times accompanied by vast crowds of supporters, clearly echo Christ's entry into Jerusalem, while his explicit gesture to banish the money-men from Novgorod parallels Christ's expulsion of the money-lenders from the Temple. Other biblical references are also clearly discernible. The fall of Pskov, for example, is symbolized by the annihilation of much of the population at the hands of the Teutonic Knights in a scene reminiscent of the Massacre of the Innocents, while Nevsky's summoning of an army of national defenders, who appear to rise up from the very earth itself, carries clear connotations of the Last Judgement. In these sequences, Eisenstein also makes reference to his own earlier films, including a brief reworking of the Odessa-steps sequence with the Teutonic Knights replacing the Tsarist guard, and a repetition of the notorious infanticide from *Strike*. The allusions to religion in *Alexander Nevsky* are, it might be added, entirely consistent with contemporary developments within official Socialist Realism and serve to reinforce the explicit parallel between Nevsky and Stalin. As many historians of Soviet culture have argued in recent years, the cultural mythologizing at play in conventional representations of the Soviet leader frequently drew heavily upon pre-Revolutionary religious ideology, presenting both Lenin and Stalin as secular saints.[23]

In the wake of the *Bezhin Meadow* scandal, it was hardly surprising that Eisenstein focused on making *Alexander Nevsky* one of his most straightforward and accessible films. Its plot is simple in structure, presenting unambiguous good guys and bad guys and an inevitable heroic resolution. He even introduced a romantic subplot through the figures of Vasily Buslai and Gavrilo Olexich, who compete for the affections of Olga, a maid from Novgorod. Despite the seriousness of the subject matter, there are also elements of comedy and farce. In the end, one might say, *Alexander Nevsky* contains something for everyone.

Perhaps the most experimental element of the film can be found in the relationship between image and sound. Despite its status as Eisenstein's first full-length sound film, *Alexander Nevsky* is notable for its relatively sparse use of dialogue, with many of the characters speaking in short, declamatory sentences. In this way, the dialogue may be read as reminiscent of the inter-titles deployed in his earlier silent films. The technical limitations of sound-recording equipment may have been a contributing factor. As James Goodwin has pointed out, much of the dialogue is delivered from a static position, while directional or perspectival sound is entirely absent.[24] Moreover, post-production musical accompaniment constitutes a significant proportion of the overall screen time. While necessity may have been at least a contributory mother of invention, Eisenstein's collaboration with Prokofiev also gave him his first major opportunity to integrate sound into the visual narration of the film. Indeed, many critics have notably compared *Alexander Nevsky* to opera, both in its musicality and in its theatricality.[25] A key example is the scene following the battle on the ice. As the camera pans over the prone bodies of the

Russian warriors lying wounded and dying on the field of conflict, women bearing torches enter from backstage, silhouetted against a projected backdrop of a dark, louring sky, metaphorically signifying a shroud. To reinforce the sense of tragedy, several of the warriors momentarily raise themselves from the ground and, with their dying breaths, call out the names of loved ones – mothers, sisters, wives or lovers never to be seen again. Accompanying this sequence is a haunting and melancholy aria which, combined with the self-conscious artificiality of the scene, recognizably shot in a studio, is clearly designed to give the impression of a stage performance far more than suggesting a real scene on a battlefield.

Other aspects of Prokofiev's score were also conceived as integral to reinforcing the narrative of Eisenstein's film. For example, the fanfares played by the Teutonic Knights are deliberately dissonant, in contrast to the harmonious music that invariably accompanies Nevsky and his retinue. Even the recording of these fanfares, played on brass instruments positioned deliberately too close to microphones, was conceived to generate distortion and thus signify negative connotations when combined with the images of the notional enemy. Yet perhaps the most innovative dialogue between sound and image comes in the scene in which Nevsky's victory is being celebrated. Here, Eisenstein had originally intended to shoot footage of Russian folk musicians to a predetermined musical score.[26] However, this decision was reversed and the footage was shot with no accompaniment. Instead Prokofiev composed the music to 'align' with the images produced by Eisenstein. Here, Prokofiev's music consciously echoes the montage effect of Eisenstein's editing so that the regular 4/4 beat is fragmented, as if the music itself has been cut at random points and reassembled to match the film footage.

While *Alexander Nevsky* undoubtedly has some key moments of innovative synthesis between sound and image, it might be argued that this falls some way short of Eisenstein's earlier ambitious claims in his 'Statement on Sound'. Nonetheless, his collaboration

'Musicians', *Alexander Nevsky*.

with Prokofiev was ultimately to have the effect of drawing him back to the stage in 1939, as well as facilitating a further collaboration between the two artists for Eisenstein's last film project, *Ivan the Terrible*.

The favourable reception of *Alexander Nevsky* brought about a significant rehabilitation of Eisenstein's reputation. In addition to the Order of Lenin and honorary doctorate bestowed upon him by the VGIK in the immediate wake of the film's release, he was also made head of productions at Mosfilm in 1940 and, the following year, awarded the Stalin Prize. New opportunities soon presented themselves. Following a brief period working on a never to be realized Civil War film, he turned his attention to a new project combining historical spectacle with modern Soviet achievements. In the late 1930s, the Soviet state launched one of its last inter-war grand construction projects: the building of a canal cutting a swath through 270 kilometres of desert to irrigate the cotton fields of Uzbekistan. The Fergana Canal project, although on a more modest scale than the White Sea Canal (1931–3) and the Moscow–Volga Canal (1932–7), drew considerable press attention as the Soviet state sought to represent the enterprise as symptomatic of a sociological shift in the southern republics from feudalism to socialism. In the summer of 1939, Pavlenko visited the site and reported back enthusiastically to Eisenstein. Within a matter of days Eisenstein himself travelled to the region, together with Tisse, to start work on a film celebrating this monumental achievement. However, Eisenstein did not simply want to make a film about present successes. Rather, in a rapidly prepared script, he constructed a historical panorama divided into three parts. The first part, set in the late fourteenth century, recounted Tamerlane's destruction of a city by flooding. Here the diversion of water was represented as a strategic weapon of tyranny. The second part, set in the early twentieth century, charted a peasant revolution against local landowners who attempted to restrict access to the water supply, while the third celebrated the successful building of the Fergana Canal in the present day. In all three episodes, the inexorable power of water as an elemental force of nature is centre stage, clearly intended to represent, metaphorically, the inexorable power of the Revolution. Between July and September of 1939, Eisenstein's team shot extensive footage of the canal project. However, lack of funds and the dwindling support of the Moscow studios prevented the project from advancing. By October it had been abandoned, with much of the footage redeployed for newsreels and other documentary purposes.

While it remains far from clear precisely why the Moscow studios pulled the plug on the Fergana Canal project, it might be noted that Eisenstein's conception of the film as a historical epic far exceeded his initial brief. The vast resources required to film the proposed historical sequences, especially on location, may have been a further factor. Perhaps most significant of all, however, was a change in the political climate. In August 1939, while Eisenstein and his team were still filming in Uzbekistan, the Soviet Union became a signatory to one of the most notorious documents of the inter-war period: the Molotov–Ribbentrop Pact.

This treaty, assuring a non-aggression policy between National Socialist Germany and the Soviet Union, effectively orchestrated an about-turn as far as recent Soviet foreign policy was concerned. Overnight, arch enemy became staunch ally. One immediate impact of this was the need to suppress previous public declarations of antagonism between the two states. Thus, *Alexander Nevsky* was instantly withdrawn from Soviet cinemas. On the more positive side, however, the German government, in a gesture of goodwill, returned the negative of *Potemkin*, the Soviets having sold their only existing copy as export material in the mid-1920s. A more substantial consequence of the new policy, however, was the launching of a programme of cultural events and exchanges between the two nations which included the commissioning of Eisenstein to direct a production of Richard Wagner's *Die Walküre* at the Bolshoi Theatre. This would represent his first return to the stage since the 1924 production of *Gas Masks*.

It is difficult to assess Eisenstein's purpose in agreeing to participate in this project. Certainly the decision to direct an opera by Germany's favourite composer as part of a Nazi–Soviet cultural programme was rife with contradictions, not least given Eisenstein's own Jewish origins and his public condemnation, just one year earlier, of the 'outrages', 'abominations' and 'atrocities' of 'Fascist aggression'.[27] Not for the first time in recent years, he was severely compromised by circumstances. For while the commission gave him an ideal opportunity to test out some of his new ideas, not least those concerning the synthesis of sound, image, colour and space into a major *Gesamtkunstwerk*, it also placed other, more troubling, demands upon him. The most notorious of these was a Radio Moscow broadcast he made in February 1940, in the midst of war in Europe, in which he spoke in German advocating cultural co-operation between the 'two great peoples'.[28] While rehearsing *Die Walküre*, Eisenstein was also working on a proposed film biography of Russia's best-known and best-loved writer, Alexander Pushkin, to be entitled *Love of a Poet*. Eisenstein wanted to make the film in colour, a technical and economic impossibility in the Soviet Union at that time, and the project was eventually shelved. In the meantime, however, events on the bigger stage were to alter his plans.

The German invasion of Soviet territory in June 1941 signalled a predictable and dramatic end to the fallacy of the Nazi–Soviet alliance. Almost immediately, the dust was blown off copies of *Alexander Nevsky* and the film returned to Soviet screens. As a new military front formed across occupied Soviet territory, the film was also screened in improvised cinemas to front-line soldiers. *Alexander Nevsky* became, once more, the acceptable face of anti-German cinematic propaganda, and Eisenstein its symbolic representative.

News of Hitler's treachery first reached Eisenstein at his dacha in Kratovo shortly after he had completed the screenplay for his latest commission: a historical account of the sixteenth-century prince of Muscovy crowned the first Tsar of Russia, Ivan the Terrible. The commission had come directly from Stalin, who was no doubt hoping for another straightforwardly heroic movie aligning the great deeds of past heroes with his own contemporary achievements. Indeed, *Alexander Nevsky* had proven to be but one of many recently completed movies celebrating Russia's past.[29] The dramatically changed circumstances brought about by the outbreak of war, however, put Eisenstein's new project temporarily on the back burner as cinema rapidly became a weapon in the conflict. During the first weeks of war, Eisenstein, as head of productions at Mosfilm, turned his hand to the production of short propaganda movies in the spirit of the early Bolshevik *agitki*. In July 1941 he also participated in an anti-Fascist meeting broadcast on American radio. This provided an opportunity for him to regain some international credibility after his earlier pro-German radio broadcast.

As Hitler's troops drew ever nearer to Moscow, a mass evacuation campaign was launched, and in October 1941, Eisenstein, along with much of the Soviet film industry, was relocated to Alma-Ata in Kazakhstan. Over the next eighteen months, while the fate of the Soviet Union was being decided on the battlefields of Kharkov, Voronezh and Stalingrad, Eisenstein worked on the script for *Ivan the Terrible*. Given the wartime conditions, shooting did not begin until April 1943, by which time he had undertaken extensive research, produced hundreds of drawings and prepared the screenplay for publication in *Novy Mir*.[30] He had also completed the casting, which once more included Cherkasov in the title role. More surprisingly, however, was the recruitment of Andrei Moskvin as cameraman. Tisse, who had worked with Eisenstein on all his previous productions, was retained, but only for the outdoor scenes.

Despite regular shortages of film stock and a limited supply of electricity, shooting continued through the rest of the year. By early 1944, it was becoming increasingly evident that the end product would significantly exceed the usual length of a feature film. Eisenstein thus gained approval to work the material into three separate films. In July he was back in Moscow to complete the editing for what was to become *Part I* of the trilogy, once more working with Prokofiev as musical director. In August this part was given its first screening before the Committee on Cinematic Affairs. Following a few revisions, including the removal of a prologue showing the childhood of Ivan (later to be reintroduced as a flashback in *Part II*), the film was approved for release in December and premiered in mid-January 1945. Throughout the rest of the year, Eisenstein continued work on *Part II*. *Ivan the Terrible, Part I* was well received in official circles and earned Eisenstein his second

Stalin Prize. Thus on 2 February 1946, the same day that he completed the editing for *Part II*, he attended an official party in honour of this award. At 2 a.m., while dancing, he collapsed and was rushed to the Kremlin hospital. He had suffered a major heart attack.

Eisenstein spent several weeks in hospital and the best part of the following year recuperating. At the same time he had to contend with yet another fateful shift in his roller-coaster career. A few days after his heart attack, *Ivan the Terrible, Part II* was given its first official screening. Reactions were far from positive, and the public release of the film was put on hold. Matters deteriorated in the late summer of 1946 when the movie was publicly criticized in an official decree issued as part of a new cultural campaign to reassert the authority of the Communist Party.[31] Eisenstein was once more forced to issue a public admission of his errors.[32] Still hopeful of completing the film, he wrote to Stalin requesting a meeting to discuss changes to the movie, and, in February 1947, together with Cherkasov, he was summoned to the Kremlin. Stalin, along with Party officials Vyacheslav Molotov and Andrei Zhdanov, condemned the movie on several counts. Firstly, it was claimed, he had represented Ivan's personal guard, the *oprichniki*, incorrectly, making them resemble the Ku Klux Klan. Secondly, Ivan himself was shown as too indecisive and dependent upon the advice of others – too like Hamlet, as Stalin reportedly claimed. Thirdly, while the highlighting of Ivan's cruelty was deemed correct, there was insufficient explanation for the necessity of his actions. Finally, the film was too mystical, too dependent on psychological interpretations.[33] Yet despite these shortcomings, Stalin invited Eisenstein to rework the film, suggesting that he take as long as he needed to ensure that it became 'a good picture'.[34] In the end, Eisenstein's poor health precluded him from returning to the film, and, like so many of his later projects, *Ivan the Terrible* remained unfinished. Whether or not Stalin calculated that this would be the likely eventuality is another matter.

'Reassembling the Tsar', *Ivan the Terrible, Part I*, 1945.

Ivan the Terrible set out to offer a new vision of one of history's most ruthless leaders, a vision in keeping with contemporary needs. *Part i* opens with the coronation of the seventeen-year-old Ivan and his declaration that his ultimate goal is the unification of Russia. Notably, he is introduced to the spectator in fragments, the camera focusing first on his crown, then on the sceptre and orb as they are placed in his hands. As Goodwin has pointed out, this reconstructed image of the Tsar offers an ironic reversal of the dismantling of the monument of Tsar Alexander *iii* in *October*.[35] Here, Eisenstein may also have been alluding to the reconstruction of the Tsar's reputation in recent Soviet historiography, in which the popular image of Ivan as monstrous, largely derived from Nikolai Karamzin's early nineteenth-century publication, *History of the Russian State*, was largely reshaped to present Ivan's reign as one of necessary authoritarianism for the good of the nation.[36] This scene also introduces Ivan's future enemies as both domestic and foreign, thus conflating the two principal themes central to both *Bezhin Meadow* and *Alexander Nevsky*. Among the retinue are Ivan's aunt Yefrosinia Staritskaya, who, it becomes clear, seeks to overthrow him and replace him with her feeble-minded son, Vladimir. The introduction of Ivan's two closest friends and allies, Fyodor Kolychev and Andrei Kurbsky, also sets the scene for later betrayals.

In the next scene Ivan is presented at a banquet in honour of his marriage to Anastasia. His joy, however, is marred when Kolychev takes his leave, abandoning the Tsar for the Church. Kurbsky, too, is seen to distance himself from Ivan, declaring that 'marriage sunders friendship'. It is also revealed that Kurbsky is secretly in love with Anastasia. The celebratory mood is further diminished when the peasant masses, provoked by Yefrosinia, storm the palace. Ivan, however, confronts this minor revolution head on, his sheer physical presence sufficient to overwhelm the masses, while his thinly veiled threat that heads will roll reveals his willingness to adopt the most brutal of strategies to bolster his leadership.

The arrival of an ambassador from Kazan shifts Ivan's authority from the threat of internal opponents to that of external enemies, and he is next shown commanding a military victory over the Tatar enemy. With the Soviet army still embroiled in conflict with German troops, Ivan's victory, achieved by both guile and force of arms, can be read as a patriotic call to arms. One might even argue that the emphasis on both cannons and wooden siege towers makes an overt reference to the important role played by tanks in the defence of Soviet territory during the battles of Stalingrad and Kursk.[37] As a consequence of his victory over the Tatars, Ivan gains two new allies, the peasant Malyuta Skuratov and the soldier Alexei Basmanov, both of whom will later become members of his personal guard. It is also during this conflict that he first expresses doubts concerning Kurbsky's loyalty.

Following the victory at Kazan, the scene reverts to the Kremlin, where Ivan has suddenly fallen ill. With the Tsar seemingly on his deathbed, a dispute erupts as to the succession. Should the crown pass to Ivan's infant son, Dmitry, or to Yefrosinia's son, Vladimir? Kurbsky, initially unwilling to commit himself to either camp, hears that Ivan has recovered and instantly declares undying loyalty to the Tsar. He is rewarded by Ivan, who elevates him to a position of greater authority. In a knowing gesture, however, Ivan simultaneously pushes Kurbsky to his knees. Whether Ivan's illness was genuine, or a ruse to test the loyalties of his retinue, is left unclear. His authority reasserted, he plans a new campaign, this time against the Poles, despite the resistance of the boyars and the Church, both of whom withhold financial support. As the scene shifts to the state room, Ivan asks his emissary to visit Queen Elizabeth I to secure Russia's continuing trade with England. He further proposes that the English strategically bypass the Baltic ports, under enemy control, and sail straight to the White Sea. Here we have another explicit reference to the contemporary situation: the importance of Great Britain's Arctic convoys during the Second World War.

Thwarted by Ivan's strategies on all sides, Yefrosinia now poisons Anastasia by mixing a potion which Ivan unwittingly hands to his bride. This treacherous murder, an attempt to destroy Ivan, has the opposite effect. On also hearing that Kurbsky has transferred his allegiance to the enemy, King Sigismund of Poland, Ivan declares that he will now form his own personal guard, the *oprichniki*, made up of those who will swear an oath of total loyalty. The first to sign up is Basmanov's own son, Fyodor, who renounces his paternal bond in favour of servitude to the Tsar. As a final leadership strategy, Ivan abdicates and retires to the monastery of Alexandrova Sloboda, calculating that the masses will call on him to return to Moscow. The film concludes with a dramatic shot of his huge profile set against the diminutive masses marching in a sinuous line across a snow-covered landscape to bow before him. As he raises his long, pointed beard and slowly lowers it again, the crowd kneels in supplication, referring to him in song as 'beloved

'Ivan in Profile', *Ivan the Terrible, Part I*.

father'. Ivan has now acquired total authority over the entire Russian population – peasants, priests and boyars alike.

The first part of *Ivan the Terrible* notably reinforces many of the familiar conventions of Socialist Realism. As in *Alexander Nevsky*, we are again presented with a powerful authoritarian figure who commands the respect of the masses. Also like Nevsky, Ivan is represented as on a journey during which he is forced to overcome a number of trials. Although Ivan's hunger for power is clearly antipathetic to the concept of collectivity, it is constantly reiterated that this is sought not for the self but 'for the sake of the Great Russian kingdom'. Unlike Nevsky, however, Ivan is shown to have a distinctly dark side to his nature. His cruelty is notably directed as much against his internal foes as against foreign invaders, although, in justification, he is presented as more sinned against than sinning. As a wartime movie, *Ivan the Terrible, Part I* extols the virtues of strong leadership, indeed the very kind of leadership that many, rightly or wrongly, ascribed to Stalin.

Part II commences with a reprise taking us up to Ivan's return to Moscow. Here he is challenged by his former friend Kolychev, who has become Filipp, Metropolitan of Moscow. In an attempt to justify his actions, Ivan recounts to Filipp episodes from his childhood, presented as a series of flashbacks. Here we learn for the first time that Ivan's mother, like his wife, was poisoned by the boyars who subsequently controlled Russia during his regency, increasing Russia's dependence on external forces. As the young Ivan matures, he begins to impose his will and proposes for the first time that Russia should determine its own future. He also commits his first act of cruelty, arresting one of the boyars for putting his feet on his dead mother's bed.

Although *Ivan the Terrible, Part II* should be read as a continuation of the larger project, the childhood scene notably introduces a dramatic shift in emphasis from *Part I*. From this point on, Ivan's actions are increasingly explained less by socio-historical circumstances than by the psychological effects upon his upbringing and his emotional state. For example, Ivan openly declares his sense of loneliness and alienation, and courts Filipp's affection and loyalty. He even succumbs to Filipp's demands that the Metropolitan be given the right to overturn Ivan's proposed punishment of members of the Kolychev family. Yet, despite having given his word, Ivan compliantly allows his right-hand man, Skuratov, to execute the Kolychevs, under the pretence that he is unaware of Skuratov's actions. When Ivan is faced with the evidence of these executions, however, his cry 'Too few' indicates that, despite claims to the contrary, he intends to extend his reign of terror. Once again the justification for his actions as outlined in *Part 1*, namely that such acts were necessary for the unification of Russia, drifts imperceptibly into the background as Ivan's sadistic and despotic character increasingly takes centre stage.

Next Eisenstein introduces a scene that may well have inspired Stalin's association of Ivan with Hamlet. Filipp seeks to humiliate Ivan by inviting him to a performance of an ancient morality play entitled *The Fiery Furnace*. Like the play-within-the-play in Shakespeare's *Hamlet*, *The Fiery Furnace* uses parable to highlight Ivan's own cruelty. The ruse fails, however, when he refuses to change his ways, declaring instead that he will live up to his sobriquet. He will indeed be Ivan the 'terrible'. With their main ally, Filipp, now under arrest, the boyars make a plan to assassinate Ivan and place Vladimir on the throne. The plot backfires, however, when Vladimir, falsely befriended and plied with drink by Ivan, foolishly reveals the plan. Ivan quickly moves not only to prevent his own assassination, but to ensure that Vladimir is killed in his place. He dresses Vladimir in the Tsar's royal garb and sends him into the cathedral, where he is stabbed to death by the assassin, who is unaware of the switch.

Like *Part 1*, the second part of *Ivan the Terrible* concludes with the Tsar declaring that his actions have been determined by his ambitions to secure a stable and unified Russian state. However, what has gone before casts grave doubts on this claim. Rather, it would seem that Ivan's cruelty has been driven less by political necessity than by his own childhood traumas and a continuing desire to maintain personal authority. In the wake of the Purges of the late 1930s and the new post-war campaign to re-impose Stalin's authority, such a presentation of tyranny was, at best, a high-risk strategy, and it is hardly surprising that the film was banned. Whether this reflected poor judgement on Eisenstein's part, or a courageous attack on the Soviet leader, is less clear. We may never know precisely what the director's intentions were.[38] Either way, it needs to be recognized that at the time of completing *Part II*, Eisenstein was still planning to work on the third part of his trilogy.

Any consideration of the third part of *Ivan the Terrible* is necessarily dependent upon the published screenplay (Eisenstein did not live to complete his trilogy), although it needs to be acknowledged that he diverged considerably from this in *Parts I* and *II*. What can be deduced, however, is that he intended to include Ivan's annihilation of the city and people of Novgorod, a scene that would surely have carried connotations for many contemporary spectators regarding the destruction of much of that city at the hands of the Germans in 1943. He also planned to end the film with Ivan, following the defeat of the Livonian army, having finally reached the shores of the Baltic, thus securing for Russia a much-coveted seaport. Once again the recent annexation of the Baltic republics, including Eisenstein's native Latvia, would certainly have carried significant contemporary resonances.

Even in its unfinished condition, *Ivan the Terrible* is one of Eisenstein's most fascinating and complex productions. As Goodwin has claimed, the film might best be considered as a 'specular drama' in which vision and the gaze play a dominant thematic role.[39] Joan Neuberger has elaborated on this concept to claim that '[e]yes are full-fledged characters in *Ivan*. They appear as objects, gestures, symbols and metaphors in almost every scene.'[40] On one

'The Importance of Eyes', *Ivan the Terrible,
Part I*.

level, this is made evident by eye movements and gestures of several of the main characters. Ivan's young wife, Anastasia, for example, is represented as having wide, innocent eyes and is frequently shown gazing up at her new husband with an expression of awe. This notably changes, however, in two scenes which mark transitions in the narrative. Firstly, during the wedding feast she is shown modestly covering her eyes as her husband gazes towards her, only to change this expression to a bold, knowingly flirtatious, sideways glance at Kurbsky, suggestive of a surreptitious return of his illicit affections. Secondly, just before her murder, as she raises the poisoned goblet gradually to cover her entire face, an expression of fear replaces innocence the instant before the goblet obscures her eyes, thus signifying her awareness of her own imminent death. In contrast, Yefrosinia's eyes constantly dart from side to side, like those of a hunted animal. Her constant, anxiety-driven vigilance thus betrays her true nature as enemy of the Tsar. Although also identified as an enemy of the Tsar, Vladimir's large, watery eyes appear to notice nothing and he is frequently shown staring vacantly into space. The innocence of Anastasia's expression is here transformed into naivety, Vladimir's mind seemingly as empty as his gaze.

Unsurprisingly, Ivan's gaze is the most forceful of all, at times even demonic. He is typically represented staring purposefully into the distance, beyond the frame of the shot and above the heads of those who surround him; a metaphor for his superiority over the masses and his clear vision of both present and future. As the film progresses, we are made increasingly aware of his inner vision, and at times his physiological sight becomes virtually redundant. For example, at the beginning of *Part 1*, he is introduced seen from the rear, turned away from the entourage attending his coronation. Yet, as the first sense of court intrigue is presented, we sense that he is fully aware of precisely what is going on, as if he has eyes in the back of his head. This notion is echoed in the final scene when he is shown in profile against the masses, his physical gestures controlling the crowd without the need for direct visual engagement. Significantly, Ivan's vision is also supplemented by those who serve him. Skuratov, for example, is constantly shown emerging from the shadows to spy on Ivan's enemies, thus effectively becoming a metaphor for Tsarist surveillance. In one notable scene, the camera zooms in ever closer on Skuratov's face as he raises an eyebrow with his finger to allow his right eye to open fully and thus witness the conspiracies being plotted against his lord and master.

Nor is vigilance confined to the characters within the narrative, for even the walls have eyes that stare down knowingly, judgementally, at the court intrigues. For example, when Kurbsky believes that Ivan will soon die, he proposes marriage to Anastasia in front of an enormous religious icon. As he promises to make Anastasia his 'Muscovy Tsarina', the camera zooms in on the huge eye of the icon, seemingly watching over this scene and thus reinforcing the notion that Ivan is aware of the action, consciously testing Kurbsky's loyalty. Similarly, at the beginning of *Part II*, much emphasis is placed upon the fearful gaze of the Angel of Wrath, depicted in a mural that covers the ceiling and walls of Ivan's throne room. As Filipp enters to challenge Ivan's tyranny over the boyars, his fiery stare is replicated in that of the angel on the wall behind him. Further, it is the angel that forges the link between past and present as it bears witness to Ivan's childhood experiences.

Yet perhaps the most significant deployment of vision and the gaze in *Ivan the Terrible* is in the allusion to the spectator's engagement with the narrative on screen. Here, the emphasis on eyes is reminiscent of Eisenstein's earliest films, such as *Strike* and *Potemkin*, where, as Neuberger has reminded us, the camera acted not as a passive spectator – the cine-eye of Vertov – but as an active tool for the reshaping of the consciousness of the masses.[41] In this context, the viewer of *Ivan the Terrible* is similarly constructed as far from passive. Like the eyes on the wall, he or she is fully implicated in the unfolding narrative, forced to make a judgement of the action taking place before his or her vision. Here the spectator is forced to confront a duality of representation. Is Ivan a self-serving monster or hero of the Russian state, and are his brutal actions those of a tyrant or of a loyal servant of the national cause? Perhaps the most troubling duality of all here is Skuratov's eye as it stares directly towards the spectator. In a climate in which constant surveillance was an everyday, and a potentially life-threatening, experience, this gesture would surely have been identified as destabilizing the sense of who was watching and who was being watched.

As Neuberger has also argued, gender identities are similarly destabilized in *Ivan the Terrible* to suggest another set of dualities. For example, Yefrosinia, though female, is presented with notably masculine features, in contrast to her feminized son, Vladimir, while the Polish court of King Sigismund is dressed in 'a parody of effeminacy: ostentatious lace-trimmed jackets and pantaloons,

'At the Polish Court', *Ivan the Terrible, Part II*, 1946.

earrings, meticulously (and ridiculously) coiffed hair'.[42] Further, both Kurbsky and Fyodor Basmanov, at various points in the narrative, are presented as fulfilling the role of surrogate wife to Ivan. These inversions, breaking down simplistic distinctions between gender identities, further echo the 'unity of opposites' that forms the central theme of the film.[43]

This notion of duality is also articulated in Eisenstein's use of shadows. During the coronation scene, for example, Ivan declares that he will be sole ruler of a united Russia. To reinforce this ambition, his face is shown in close-up with the shadow of a double-headed eagle, cast by his sceptre, emblazoned on his cheek. Yet, even as this shot visually articulates his dominant leadership, voices are heard among the assembled crowd to challenge the legitimacy of his authority. Further, as Yuri Tsivian has pointed out, Eisenstein's use of shadows in the state-room scene is integral to our understanding of the duality of Ivan's personality. Here, as the director himself noted, the shadows projected onto the wall reflect Ivan's 'outer ego'.[44] Thus, the shadow of an astrological sphere above his head signifies 'a maze of his cosmic world thoughts', while the scale disparities between his shadow and that of his envoy 'reflects the genuine difference in scale between two characters which normally would appear identically dimensioned'.[45]

Shadows are also deployed to add a darker, more sinister mood to the interior scenes. Thus, dramatic lighting generates a constant sense of dark, hidden recesses and sudden, sinister apparitions. One of the most striking of these is the disturbing appearance of a shadow descending a staircase at the precise moment when Yefrosinia warns Kurbsky that he is a marked man. At first glance, the shadow appears to be Ivan's, but it is then revealed to be Skuratov's, emphasizing once more the duality of appearances. Here, Eisenstein also seems to be quoting directly from F. W. Murnau's gothic horror classic *Nosferatu* (1922), and not just in visual terms. The suggestion, for example, that Skuratov and Ivan

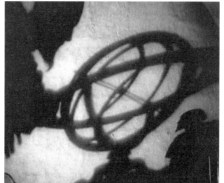

'Shadows', *Ivan the Terrible, Part 1.*

can be one and the same person and that this dual being might be read as a monster in the same vein as Murnau's evil creature adds richness to this cinematic quotation. Nor is this the sole reference to German Expressionist cinema within *Ivan the Terrible*. For example, to reinforce the notion that Vladimir is feeble-minded, he is shown catching a fly, a notable parallel to the scene of the madman imprisoned in a mental asylum in Robert Wiene's *The Cabinet of Dr Caligari* (1919).

Nor is it just these isolated quotations that link *Ivan the Terrible* to an Expressionist aesthetic. More particularly, the sharply defined lighting and steep camera angles generate an anxiety-inducing, claustrophobic sense of compressed space more akin to a dungeon or asylum than to a royal palace.[46] Here, Eisenstein's decision to deploy Moskvin in preference to Tisse for the interior scenes suggests a strong desire to find a new visual aesthetic for the *Ivan* project. Similarly, the spiky, elongated forms of decorative objects reinforces the link between the gothic and an early twentieth-century Expressionist aesthetic, while even the characters themselves, with their exaggerated costumes and physical gestures, lend *Ivan the Terrible* a visual appearance dramatically distinct from other Soviet movies of its time.

Another key element that helped to further this distinctiveness and forge a direct link to an Expressionist aesthetic was Eisenstein's first use of colour. In late 1945 he acquired a limited quantity of colour film stock, war booty from the Agfa factory in Germany. As he had long been interested in the possibilities of colour in film, he used this to shoot one of the final scenes of *Ivan the Terrible, Part II*, the dance sequence in the banquet hall. Much as his earlier theories had advocated the deployment of sound as an integral aspect of cinematic montage, Eisenstein now aimed to use colour in a similar manner. Therefore, rather than emphasize the naturalistic colours of a given scene, he sought to combine colour with image and sound to create an overall synthesis of narration, mood and sensation. So, in the banquet scene he used colour specifically to highlight the carnivalistic sense of frenzy, energy and danger that accompanied Ivan's discovery of the boyars' plot to assassinate him and his own improvised murder of Vladimir. The scene commences with a veritable explosion of colour and movement, the whole accompanied by Prokofiev's raucous music. Golds, reds, blues and blacks merge before each tonality gives way, in turn, to another. As Eisenstein later indicated, gold signified 'a festive, regal theme' and was here associated with the costumes of Ivan and Vladimir, while '[t]he red supplies an ominous theme and acts as blood'.[47]

To highlight this more symbolic use of colour, Eisenstein used red as the dominant tonality in the scene in which Ivan castigates Basmanov, reminding him that he is not linked by blood to the royal family. As Basmanov responds, conspiratorially, that he and the Tsar are linked by the closer bond of the blood they have spilled together, a sinister blood-red shadow is cast across their faces, signifying their past deeds and foreshadowing Ivan's execution of Basmanov in the proposed *Part III*. Similarly, as Ivan's plan to murder Vladimir unfolds, the tonality of the scene shifts to blue, then to black, to signal what is to come. Vladimir's awareness of the fate about to befall him is also signalled by a colour transition as his face, brightly lit against a dark blue background, is suddenly cast in shadow only to reappear shaded in a ghostly blue, as if all the blood has drained from his visage. As Eisenstein later wrote, colour should have its own emotional value, connected with a precise idea.'[48]

As David Bordwell has pointed out, Eisenstein's use of colour for the banquet scene in *Ivan the Terrible, Part II* has 'the air of a theoretical experiment', and suggests future directions he may well have taken had circumstances allowed.[49] Indeed, in late 1946, he was invited to make a full-length colour film to celebrate the 800th anniversary of the founding of Moscow. For the project he planned to film seven episodes, each assigned a specific colour of the rainbow. Sadly, the film was never made. Throughout 1947 he continued to work on several book projects, including his memoirs and a history of Soviet film. Both remained unfinished. In June he was also made a director of the Cinema section of the Institute for Art History at the Academy of Sciences.[50] The innovative possibilities of colour in film, however, were never far from his thinking, and during this period he also worked on several essays on the theme. In early February 1948, just a couple of weeks after celebrating his fiftieth birthday, he was at his desk, writing a letter to Kuleshov in which he outlined his latest theories on colour, when he suffered a second major heart attack. The next morning his body was found lying on the floor of his flat.

Epilogue

Eisenstein's career underwent many transformations. During the 1920s, for example, he was widely regarded as one of the most important directors of the age only to see his reputation plummet, in the Soviet Union at least, following critical reactions to *October*. He remained largely out of favour for the next decade until the release of *Alexander Nevsky* relaunched both his career and his standing among the Soviet cultural elite. For the next eight years Eisenstein was once again lauded as the pre-eminent figure in Soviet cinematography only to see his star wane once more, following the official criticism and banning of *Ivan the Terrible, Part II*. This cycle of peaks and troughs continued even after his death. During the last years of Stalin's rule, Eisenstein was officially regarded as a director who had never truly fulfilled his potential, corrupted by his bourgeois-inspired fascination with individualism and formalism. However, in the cultural thaw that followed Nikita Khrushchev's 1956 denunciation of Stalin, Eisenstein was once more celebrated, and both his films and writings began to acquire canonical status.

Throughout this period, Eisenstein's status as one of early cinema's guiding lights was also beginning to be recognized in the West. In Europe and the United States, *Potemkin, October* and *Alexander Nevsky* were widely screened and regarded by many as masterpieces of world cinema. Eisenstein's reputation was also bolstered by the work of scholars including Jay Leyda, Ivor Montagu,

The last photograph of Sergei Eisenstein.

Léon Moussinac and Marie Seton, each of whom drew increasing attention to his cinematic endeavours, his life history and his theoretical writings. This resurrection perhaps reached its apogee in 1958. At the Brussels World's Fair, the sixtieth anniversary of Eisenstein's birth was celebrated with the official world premiere of *Ivan the Terrible, Part II* while a panel of international critics voted *Potemkin* the greatest film of all time.

Over the next two decades, Eisenstein's reputation continued to wax and wane. During the 1960s, for example, in the midst of Cold War tensions, his notional accommodation of Stalinism began to be increasingly scrutinized in both the East and the West.[1] Further, his emphasis on the importance of montage also began to fall out of favour following a significant shift in cinematographic conventions, largely inspired by the writings of André Bazin, the influential editor of the French film journal *Cahiers du cinéma*. For Bazin, montage highlighted the artificiality and manipulation he regarded as anathema to successful film-making. Instead he championed continuity, the long shot and the notional 'invisibility' of the director. For Bazin and his followers, the films of Jean Renoir, Orson Welles and the Italian Neo-Realists exemplified cinema at its very best. This left little room for Eisenstein.

By the 1970s, however, Eisenstein's international reputation began to rise to prominence once more. As Film Studies gradually expanded as an academic discipline, scholars increasingly looked back to the early Soviet period as vital to an understanding of the history of cinema. This interest was further bolstered by studies of wider cultural activities in the early Bolshevik period, not least the work and theories of the Constructivists, the LEF group and other members of the Soviet avant-garde. All of this provided a wider context in which Eisenstein's films and writings could be examined. The publication, in the Soviet Union, of the six-volume edition of his writings, later translated into numerous languages, provided further impetus for scholarly engagement with, and analysis of, his oeuvre.

In the last decade or so, interests in early Soviet cinema have gradually shifted away from the canonical works of the best-known directors towards adopting a more bottom-up approach focusing predominantly on the 'popular' films beloved by audiences. This history of 'forgotten' Soviet cinema has helped to unearth some truly fascinating material worthy of study in its own right and has also helped to transform our understanding of the breadth and diversity of early Soviet filmmaking.[2] It has also provided a wonderfully enriched context in which we can reassess the work of Eisenstein and other well-known Soviet filmmakers of the same period.

It should be noted, in conclusion, that the impact of Eisenstein's legacy on world cinema has been immense, and continues to be felt to this day. Even the most cursory list of directors whose work has clearly been influenced by him would include Kenneth Anger, Ingmar Bergman, Robert Bresson, Luis Buñuel, Federico Fellini, Jean-Luc Godard, Peter Greenaway, John Grierson, Alfred Hitchcock, Derek Jarman, Akira Kurosawa, Chris Marker, Pier Paolo Pasolini, Michael Powell and Emeric Pressburger, Satyajit Ray, Alain Resnais, Ken Russell, Martin Scorsese and François Truffaut. Specific references to famous Eisenstein sequences have also turned up in some seemingly unlikely places, from reworkings of the Odessa-steps sequence in Woody Allen's *Bananas* (1971) and Brian De Palma's *The Untouchables* (1987) to a historically reconfigured battle on the ice in Antoine Fuqua's recent block-buster *King Arthur* (2004). Eisenstein's notion of sound/image counterpoint was also compellingly explored in such cinematic masterpieces as Carol Reed's *The Third Man* (1949), Stanley Kubrick's *2001: A Space Odyssey* (1968) and Francis Ford Coppola's *Apocalypse Now* (1979).

In late and post-Soviet Russian filmmaking, the dominant influence of Andrei Tarkovsky might seem to suggest that Eisenstein's legacy has been little embraced. After all, Tarkovsky's emphasis on the long shot, slow pace and relative inaction seems to stand at the opposite pole to Eisenstein's dynamic montage. Yet, as some scholars have recently suggested, Tarkovsky's seemingly strict opposition to Eisensteinian cinema perhaps embraces as much as it rejects and might be read as a kind of inverted homage to his predecessor.[3] As Vida T. Johnson has put it, 'Despite Tarkovsky's protestations and critiques of Eisenstein's films, it is hard to imagine *Andrei Rublev* without *Ivan the Terrible*.'[4] Alexander Sokurov's more recent, and widely acclaimed, *Russian Ark* (2002) might similarly be seen as overtly acknowledging the legendary status of Eisenstein. Sokurov's decision to set his film exclusively in the Winter Palace inevitably recalls Eisenstein's *October*, while his emphasis on celebrating pre-Revolutionary history invites the viewer to consider *Russian Ark* as a conscious remaking, perhaps even a corrective, of Eisenstein's classic for a new, post-Soviet age. Further, Sokurov's decision to shoot the entire movie in one continuous take, therefore removing the need for any editing, must surely be read as a direct riposte to Eisenstein's stress on the importance

Sergei Eisenstein posing on the Tsar's throne in the Winter Palace.

of montage. Thus, in both his own backyard and the wider global village, Eisenstein's legacy has cast a long shadow over filmmaking and will, no doubt, continue to do so in the future.

In 1962, the Soviet dissident writer Alexander Solzhenitsyn famously made reference to Eisenstein in his highly influential novel *One Day in the Life of Ivan Denisovich*. In one of two separate mentions, Solzhenitsyn provocatively introduced a debate between camp prisoners regarding the merits of *Ivan the Terrible*. For one prisoner, Eisenstein was the supreme artist whose work transcended time and place. 'If one is to be objective', he argued, 'one must acknowledge that Eisenstein is a genius.' The second prisoner, however, challenged this view, stating that Eisenstein produced 'spice and poppy-seed instead of everyday bread and butter!' He continued, 'Don't call him genius! Call him an arse-licker, obeying a vile dog's order. Geniuses don't adjust their interpretations to suit the taste of tyrants.'[5] Here, Solzhenitsyn proposed two views of Eisenstein, thesis and antithesis, though in the context of the post-Stalinist thaw of the early 1960s, it seems clear that he was favouring the second reading. Yet, in a post-Soviet era when so much has been done to re-examine and reassess the role of official Stalinist culture, it is, perhaps, a synthesis of these notions that best reflects the reality of Eisenstein's career. Yes, Eisenstein did indeed serve the Stalinist regime, and, despite major setbacks, he gained many rewards for this service. Its nature, however, cannot be reduced to simplistic propagandistic support or subtle Aesopian resistance. It was, if anything, both of these things, sometimes even at the same time. And it is precisely the subtlety, complexity and sheer richness of his negotiation of such a difficult path that has allowed Eisenstein's works to continue to speak so eloquently.

References

Prologue

1 Sergei Eisenstein, *Beyond the Stars: The Memoirs of Sergei Eisenstein*, ed. Richard Taylor, trans. William Powell (London, 1995), p. 507.
2 Eisenstein, *Beyond the Stars*, p. 507.
3 Oksana Bulgakowa, *Sergei Eisenstein: A Biography* (Berlin and San Francisco, CA, 1998), p. x.
4 Eisenstein, *Beyond the Stars*, pp. 75–7.
5 Bulgakowa, *Sergei Eisenstein*, p. x.
6 Eisenstein, *Beyond the Stars*, p. 507.
7 Ibid.

1 Experimentation

1 For an account of the Russian presence in Paris during this period, see D. A. Gutnov, 'Young Russians in Paris 1900–1910: A Social Approach to the History of Russian Emigration', in *Sotsialnaya Istoriya Ezhegodnik* (Moscow, 2004).
2 Eisenstein later described his father as 'one of the most flowery representatives of that architectural decadence – *style moderne*'. See Sergei Eisenstein, *Beyond the Stars: The Memoirs of Sergei Eisenstein*, ed. Richard Taylor, trans. William Powell (London, 1995), p. 125.
3 David Kirby, *The Baltic World 1772–1993: Europe's Northern Periphery in an Age of Change* (London and New York, 1995) p. 228.
4 Eisenstein, *Beyond the Stars*, p. 99.
5 Ibid., p. 433.

6 Konstantin Rudnitsky, *Russian and Soviet Theatre: Tradition and the Avant Garde* (London, 1988), p. 9.

7 Ibid., pp. 9–10.

8 Eisenstein, *Beyond the Stars*, p. 550.

9 Denise Youngblood, *The Magic Mirror: Moviemaking in Russia, 1908–1918* (Madison, WI, 1999), p. 8.

10 Ibid., p. 10.

11 Richard Taylor and Ian Christie, eds, *The Film Factory: Russian and Soviet Cinema in Documents 1896–1939* (London and New York, 1988), p. 19. One might regard this attitude as somewhat disingenuous, however, when noting that the last Tsar was eager to bestow the St Stanislav Cross, second degree, upon the film producer Alexander Khanzhonkov for *The Defence of Sevastopol*. By 1915, the patriotic message of this movie, made two years earlier, was seen as of real propaganda potential to the state. See Youngblood, *Magic Mirror*, p. 28.

12 For a list of the productions Eisenstein attended, see Ronald Bergan, *Sergei Eisenstein: A Life in Conflict* (London, 1997), pp. 50–51.

13 Eisenstein, *Beyond the Stars*, p. 543.

14 Oksana Bulgakowa, *Sergei Eisenstein: A Biography* (Berlin and San Francisco, CA, 1998), p. 9.

15 Eisenstein, *Beyond the Stars*, p. 67.

16 Bulgakowa, *Sergei Eisenstein*, p. 15.

17 Lynn Mally, *Culture of the Future: The Prolekult Movement in Revolutionary Russia* (Berkeley, CA, 1990), p. xix.

18 Ibid., pp. xv–xxix.

19 Bergan, *Sergei Eisenstein*, p. 58.

20 Yeliseyev later participated as costume designer on Eisenstein's production of *Alexander Nevsky*. See Bulgakowa, *Sergei Eisenstein*, p. 196.

21 Rudnitsky, *Russian and Soviet Theatre*, p. 41.

22 Ibid., p. 44.

23 Ibid., p. 41.

24 František Déak, 'Blue Blouse (1923–1928)', *Drama Review*, XVII/1 (1973), pp. 35–46.

25 See James Riordan, *Sport in Soviet Society* (Cambridge, 1977), p. 79.

26 Jack London's short story 'The Mexican' was first published in the *Saturday Evening Post* on 19 August 1911.

27 Vladimir Tolstoy, Irina Bibikova and Catherine Cooke, *Street Art of the Revolution: Festivals and Celebrations in Russia, 1918–33* (London, 1990), p. 66.

28 Quoted in Yon Barna, *Eisenstein: The Growth of a Cinematic Genius* (London, 1973), p. 50.

29 Grigori Kozintsev *et al.*, 'Eccentrism', in Taylor and Christie, *Film Factory*, p. 59.

30 Eisenstein, *Beyond the Stars*, p. 446.

31 Rudnitsky, *Russian and Soviet Theatre*, pp. 116–17.

32 Daniel Gerould, 'Eisenstein's Wiseman', *Drama Review*, XVIII/1 (1974), p. 96.

33 When Eisenstein decided to deploy film in *Wise Man*, he sought training in the use of this new technology from the Goskino studio. Notably, Vertov was assigned to train him, but had little time or appetite for the task. Eisenstein later claimed, 'After watching us take our first two or three shots, Vertov gave us up as a hopeless case and left us to our own fate'. Quoted in Bergan, *Sergei Eisenstein*, p. 86.

34 Mel Gordon, 'Eisenstein's Later Work at the Proletkult', *Drama Review*, XXII/3 (1978), pp. 107–12.

35 Donna Oliver, 'Theatre Without the Theatre: Proletkult at the Gas Factory', *Canadian Slavonic Papers*, XXXVI/3–4 (1994), pp. 303–16.

36 The adoption of names inspired by politics or industry, such as Iskra (Spark) and Ninel (Lenin spelled backwards), was a common feature of the early Soviet period. See Sheila Fitzpatrick, *Everyday Stalinism, Ordinary Life in Extraordinary Times: Soviet Russia in the 1930s* (Oxford, 1999), pp. 83–4.

37 Nina Tumarkin, *Lenin Lives!: The Lenin Cult in Soviet Russia* (Cambridge, MA, 1983), p. 140.

38 Rudnitsky, *Russian and Soviet Theatre*, p. 103.

39 Oliver, 'Theatre Without the Theatre', p. 314.

2 Consolidation

1 Sergei Eisenstein, *Beyond the Stars: The Memoirs of Sergei Eisenstein*, ed. Richard Taylor, trans. William Powell (London, 1995), p. 16.

2 Sergei Eisenstein, *Selected Works*, I: *Writings, 1922–34*, ed. and trans. Richard Taylor (London, 1988), p. 34.

3 Ibid.

4 Ibid.

5 Ibid.

6 Ibid.

7 Richard Taylor and Ian Christie, eds, *The Film Factory: Russian and Soviet Cinema in Documents 1896–1939* (London and New York, 1988), p. 57. The Lenin quotation also appears in an article published the previous year, 'Proletkino: Quasi-Thesis', in Taylor and Christie, *Film Factory*, p. 84.

8 Taylor and Christie, *Film Factory*, p. 57.

9 This divide has been characterized by Denise Youngblood as the 'entertainment or enlightenment debate'. See Denise Youngblood, *Movies for the Masses: Popular Cinema and Soviet Society in the 1920s* (Cambridge, 1992), pp. 35–49.

10 Taylor and Christie, *Film Factory*, p. 69.

11 Ibid.

12 Ibid., p. 71.

13 Youngblood claims that foreign movies were more popular in the provinces than in Moscow. See Youngblood, *Movies for the Masses*, pp. 52–3.

14 Ibid., pp. 20, 50–67.

15 Ibid., p. 20.

16 For an analysis of these two movies, see Mike O'Mahony, 'Aelita', and Ian Christie, 'The Extraordinary Adventures of Mr West in the Land of the Bolsheviks', in Birgit Beumers, ed., *The Cinema of Russia and the Former Soviet Union* (London, 2007), pp. 25–45.

17 Sergei Eisenstein, *Film Form: Essays in Film Theory*, ed. and trans. Jay Leyda (New York, 1949), p. 11.

18 The episodes were: Geneva–Russia; Underground; May Day; 1905; Strike; Prison Riots and Escapes; October. See Jay Leyda, *Kino: A History of the Russian and Soviet Film* (New York, 1960), p. 181.

19 Viktor Shklovsky, 'Strike', in Ian Christie and John Gillett, eds, *Futurism, Formalism, FEKS: 'Eccentrism' and Soviet Cinema 1918–36* (London, 1978), p. 34.

20 Quoted in Oksana Bulgakowa, *Sergei Eisenstein: A Biography* (Berlin and San Francisco, CA, 1998), p. 53.

21 Ibid.

22 The fact that Vertov's own *Kino-Glaz* was only awarded a silver medal doubtless pleased Eisenstein immensely and further contributed to the growing animosity between the two filmmakers.

23 See the open letters exchanged between Eisenstein and Pletnyov in Jay Leyda, ed., *Eisenstein 2: A Premature Celebration of Eisenstein's Centenary* (London, 1988), pp. 1–8.

24 James Goodwin, *Eisenstein, Cinema and History* (Urbana and Chicago, 1993), p. 57.

25 Georges Sadoul, 'Interview with G. V. Alexandrov', in Herbert Marshall, ed., *The Battleship Potemkin* (New York, 1978), p. 70.

26 Quoted in Leyda, *Kino*, p. 198.

27 Marshall, *Battleship Potemkin*, p. 94.

28 Taylor and Christie, *Film Factory*, p. 140.

29 Marshall, *Battleship Potemkin*, p. 98.

30 Ibid., p. 99.

31 Ibid., p. 98.

32 Ibid., p. 101.

33 See Sergei Eisenstein, 'The Twelve Apostles', in Eisenstein, *Beyond the Stars*, pp. 153–80.

34 Eisenstein, *Beyond the Stars*, p. 175.

35 David Bordwell, *The Cinema of Eisenstein* (London, 2005), p. 70.

36 Sergei Eisenstein, 'Constanta, (Whither the Battleship Potemkin)', in Eisenstein, *Selected Works*, I, p. 67.

37 Sergei Eisenstein, 'The Montage of Film Attractions', in Eisenstein, *Selected Works*, I, p. 39.

38 Eisenstein, *Selected Works*, I, p. 67.

39 Quoted in Yuri Tsivian's commentary on the DVD of *Strike* (Eureka Video, 2000).

40 In his memoirs, Eisenstein recalled that the advice to use animals in his drawings came from an engineering colleague of his father, one Mr Afrosimov. See Eisenstein, *Beyond the Stars*, p. 576.

41 Eisenstein, *Beyond the Stars*, p. 167.

42 Herbert Marshall, 'The Puzzle of the Three Stone Lions', in Marshall, *Battleship Potemkin*, pp. 264–75.

43 Bordwell, *The Cinema of Eisenstein*, p. 54.

44 Eisenstein, *Selected Works*, I, p. 69.

45 See Vance Kepley, 'Intolerance and the Soviets: A Historical Investigation', in Ian Christie and Richard Taylor, eds, *Eisenstein Rediscovered* (London, 1993).

46 Sergei Eisenstein, *Film Form: Essays in Film Theory*, ed. and trans. Jay Leyda (New York, 1949), p. 201. *Intolerance* was first shown in the Soviet Union in 1919 and was instantly embraced by many in the Soviet film industry as an exemplary production. As Jay Leyda has pointed out, a great deal of mythology surrounds the early Soviet reception of *Intolerance.* It is reputed, for example, that on seeing the film, Lenin personally arranged for it to be screened throughout the country. Further, he is said to have invited Griffith to Russia to take control of the film industry. Whatever the truth of this might be, Griffith certainly never went. See Leyda, *Kino*, pp. 142–3.

47 Bergan, *Sergei Eisenstein*, p. 35.

48 One contemporary reviewer of Bauer's films commented on this excessive use of columns: 'Columns, columns and more columns . . . columns in the drawing room, by the fire in the office, columns here there and everywhere.' Quoted in Rachel Morley, 'Zhizn' za zhizn', in Beumers, *Cinema of Russia*, p. 17.

49 Christina Lodder, *Russian Constructivism* (New Haven, CT, and London, 1983), p. 104.

50 'Declaration of the Association of Revolutionary Russia, 1922', in John Bowlt, *Russian Art of the Avant-Garde: Theory and Criticism, 1902–1934* (London, 1988), p. 266.

51 Eisenstein, *Selected Works*, I, p. 68.

52 Ibid.

53 Ibid., p. 69 (italics in original).

54 Ibid., p. 69.

3 Transition

1 Sergei Eisenstein, *Beyond the Stars: The Memoirs of Sergei Eisenstein*, ed. Richard Taylor, trans. William Powell (London, 1995), p. 16.

2 Sergei Eisenstein, *Selected Works*, I: *Writings, 1922–34*, ed. and trans. Richard Taylor (London, 1988), pp. 44–5.

3 The resolution permitting the film to be released is reprinted in Herbert Marshall, ed., *The Battleship Potemkin* (New York, 1978), pp. 119–21.

4 Marshall, *Battleship Potemkin*, p. 145.

5 Eisenstein, *Beyond the Stars*, p. 179.

6 Quoted in Yon Barna, *Eisenstein: The Growth of a Cinematic Genius* (London, 1973), p. 111.

7 Marshall, *Battleship Potemkin*, p. 134.

8 Marshall, *Battleship Potemkin*, p. 150.

9 Quoted in Ronald Bergan, *Sergei Eisenstein: A Life in Conflict* (London, 1997), p. 118.

10 Marshall, *Battleship Potemkin*, p. 187.

11 Directed by Sergei Komarov, *The Kiss of Mary Pickford* was released in 1927 by Mezhrabpom.

12 Eisenstein, *Beyond the Stars*, p. 16.

13 One of the most striking features of the production of *Roar China!* was the stage set, featuring the bridge of a vast battleship bearing more than a passing resemblance to sequences in *Potemkin*. When, in the culminating scene, the massive ship moved towards the audience, its guns pointing directly into the auditorium, comparisons between the two productions were inevitable.

14 Oksana Bulgakowa, *Sergei Eisenstein: A Biography* (Berlin and San Francisco, CA, 1998), p. 70.

15 Dziga Vertov was commissioned to make the documentary *The Eleventh Year*. Esfir Shub produced *The Great Way* and *The Fall of the Romanov Dynasty*.

16 Richard Taylor and Ian Christie, eds, *The Film Factory: Russian and Soviet Cinema in Documents 1896–1939* (London and New York, 1988), p. 173.

17 Eisenstein, *Selected Works*, I, p. 101.

18 Sergei Eisenstein, 'Notes for a Film of *Capital*', trans. Maciej Sliwowski, Jay Leyda and Annette Michelson, *October*, II (1976), p. 3.

19 Ibid., p. 4.

20 Ibid., p. 3.

21 Mike O'Mahony, 'Bringing Down the Tsar: "Deconstructing" the Monument to Alexander III in Sergei Eisenstein's October', *Sculpture Journal*, XV/2 (2007), p. 278.

22 Richard Taylor, 'Introduction', in Eisenstein, *Selected Works*, I, pp. 4, 10. It is also tempting to speculate that the process of reconstructing the plaster replica of Opekushin's monument on its original site, a full decade after the Revolution, may have inspired Eisenstein's decision to redeploy this footage later in the film. When the pro-monarchist General Kornilov is introduced as a threat to the February Revolution, Eisenstein notably intersplices shots of the monument's fall in reverse, the Tsar thus seeming to be reassembled and resurrected to symbolize the potential political reversion to Tsarism.

23 Yuri Tsivian, 'Eisenstein and Russian Symbolist Culture: An Unknown Script of October', in Ian Christie and Richard Taylor, eds, *Eisenstein Rediscovered* (London, 1993).

24 Eisenstein, *Selected Works*, I, pp. 104–5.

25 Ibid., p. 194.

26 The story of Horatius' heroic defence of the Pons Sublicius against the entire Etruscan army was immortalized in Macauley's poem of 1881, published in *The Lays of Ancient Rome*.

27 Taylor and Christie, *Film Factory*, p. 200.

28 Ibid., p. 216.

29 Ibid., pp. 216–17.

30 Ibid., p. 230.

31 Ibid., p. 182.

32 Ibid., pp. 219–20.

33 Ibid., p. 207.

34 Ibid., p. 257.

35 Ibid.

36 Vance Kepley, 'The Evolution of Eisenstein's "Old and New"', *Cinema Journal*, XIV/1 (1974), p. 40.

37 Ibid., p. 40.

38 Eisenstein and Alexandrov highlighted this link between Lapkina and the sun in *The Old and the New*, pointing out in 'An Experiment Intelligible to the Millions' that 'a hero figures for the first time . . . our hero – our "star" – the sun.' See Taylor and Christie, *Film Factory*, p. 254.

39 Later, this topos is repeated when Lapkina casts her gaze on a tractor driver, bathing his face in a blinding light.

40 Cited in Lazar Kaganovich, *Socialist Reconstruction of Moscow and Other Cities in the USSR* (London, 1931), p. 98.

41 Denise Youngblood, *Movies for the Masses: Popular Cinema and Soviet Society in the 1920s* (Cambridge, 1992), p. 74.

42 The train reference may also be an allusion to Buster Keaton's *The General*, released just two years earlier.

4 Hiatus

1 Sergei Eisenstein, *Selected Works*, I: *Writings, 1922–34*, ed. and trans. Richard Taylor (London, 1988), p. 113.

2 Ibid., p. 114.

3 Ibid.

4 Ibid., pp. 115–22.

5 Ibid., p. 118.

6 Ibid.

7 Ibid., p. 113.

8 Oksana Bulgakowa, *Sergei Eisenstein: A Biography* (Berlin and San Francisco, CA, 1998), p. 94.

9 Marie Seton, *Sergei M. Eisenstein: A Biography* (London, 1952).

10 Ibid., p. 149.

11 Ibid., p. 145.

12 The phrase '*vieille romance russe*' appears in the opening titles of the original French version of the film.

13 Bulgakowa, *Sergei Eisenstein*, p. 103.

14 Ibid.

15 Ibid., p. 106; Ronald Bergan, *Sergei Eisenstein: A Life in Conflict* (London, 1997), p. 182.

16 Sergei Eisenstein, *Beyond the Stars: The Memoirs of Sergei Eisenstein*, ed. Richard Taylor, trans. William Powell (London, 1995), p. 245.

17 Ibid., p. 198.

18 Ibid., p. 192.

19 Eisenstein cites reports in both *Le Matin* and *Izvestiya*. See Eisenstein, *Beyond the Stars*, pp. 192, 256.

20 Pease's quotations come from a telegram sent to the head of Paramount, Jesse L. Lasky, which was published in the *Motion Picture Herald*. See Seton, *Sergei M. Eisenstein*, p. 167.

21 Ivor Montagu, *With Eisenstein in Hollywood* (New York, 1967), pp. 102–5, 345.

22 Eisenstein's scenario for *Sutter's Gold* is reproduced in Montagu, *With Eisenstein*, pp. 151–206.

23 Montagu, *With Eisenstein*, p. 113.

24 William Harrison Richardson, *Mexico Through Russian Eyes, 1806–1940* (Pittsburgh, PA, 1988), pp. 127–40.

25 John Reed, *Insurgent Mexico* (New York, 1914); Anita Brenner, *Idols Behind Altars* (New York, 1929).

26 Harry M. Geduld and Ronald Gottesman, eds, *Sergei Eisenstein and Upton Sinclair: The Making and Unmaking of Que Viva Mexico!* (Bloomington, IN, and London, 1970), p. 22.

27 Eisenstein, *Beyond the Stars*, p. 49

28 Geduld and Gottesman, *Sergei Eisenstein and Upton Sinclair*, p. 44.

29 Desmond Rochfort, *Mexican Muralists: Orozco, Rivera, Siqueiros* (London, 1993), p. 34.

30 Bulgakowa, *Sergei Eisenstein*, p. 141.

31 Geduld and Gottesman, *Sergei Eisenstein and Upton Sinclair*, pp. 284–5; Bulgakowa, *Sergei Eisenstein*, p. 137.

32 Vladimir Paperny, *Architecture in the Age of Stalin: Culture Two* (Cambridge, 2002), p. 47.

33 Geduld and Gottesman, *Sergei Eisenstein and Upton Sinclair*, p. 212.

34 More recently, in 1998, the Russian director Oleg Kovalov used Eisenstein's footage to produce *Mexican Fantasy*, an idiosyncratic film that makes no attempt to reconstruct a film that was never made.

35 Seton, *Sergei M. Eisenstein*, p. 504.

36 Richardson, *Mexico Through Russian Eyes*, p. 165.

37 Seton, *Sergei M. Eisenstein*, p. 507.

38 Ibid., p. 197.

39 Ibid., p. 508.

40 Bulgakowa, *Sergei Eisenstein*, p. 131.

41 *Diego Rivera, A Retrospective*, exh. cat. (Hayward Gallery, London, 1987).

42 See Betty Ann Brown, 'The Past Idealized: Diego Rivera's Use of Pre-Columbian Imagery', in *Diego Rivera*, pp. 139–56.

43 Desmond Rochfort, *The Murals of Diego Rivera* (London, 1987), pp. 54–5.

44 In 1922, several of the young mural painters even formed their own union. See Rochfort, *The Murals*, p. 24.

45 The less rigidly defined framing of murals, in which images frequently spilled out into alcoves and interstices, or ran up staircases and onto ceilings, would also have appealed enormously to Eisenstein. In September 1930, shortly before leaving for Mexico, he had delivered a lecture in Hollywood in which he had begun to explore the notion of breaking out beyond the conventional frame of the cinema screen. Although he specifically cited the notional boundlessness of Japanese landscape woodcuts as his primary example, the non-conventional boundaries of mural painting may also have been in the back of his mind. See 'The Dynamic Square', in Eisenstein, *Selected Works*, I, p. 207.

46 Geduld and Gottesman, *Sergei Eisenstein and Upton Sinclair*, p. 149.

47 Eisenstein, *Beyond the Stars*, p. 415.

48 Brenner, *Idols Behind Altars*, p. 190.

49 Ibid., p. 185.

50 Sarah M. Lowe, *Tina Modotti and Edward Weston: The Mexico Years* (London, 2004).

51 See Paul Rotha, Review of *Thunder Over Mexico*, quoted in Geduld and Gottesman, *Sergei Eisenstein and Upton Sinclair*, p. 415.

5 Reprieve

1 Denise Youngblood, *Movies for the Masses: Popular Cinema and Soviet Society in the 1920s* (Cambridge, 1992), p. 20.

2 David L. Hoffmann, *Peasant Metropolis: Social Identities in Moscow, 1929–41* (Ithaca, NY, and London, 1994), p. 7.

3 Oksana Bulgakowa, *Sergei Eisenstein: A Biography* (Berlin and San Francisco, CA, 1998), p. 151.

4 Directed by Grigory and Sergei Vasiliyev, *Chapayev* was released in November 1934 and rapidly became one of the most popular movies of the time, selling over 50 million tickets. See Peter Kenez, *Cinema and Soviet Society: From the Revolution to the Death of Stalin* (London, 2001), p. 155.

5 Richard Taylor and Ian Christie, eds, *The Film Factory: Russian and Soviet Cinema in Documents 1896–1939* (London and New York, 1988), p. 345.

6 Among those given higher honours were Alexandrov, Dovzhenko, Ermler, Kozintsev, Pudovkin, Trauberg and Vertov.

7 Catriona Kelly, *Comrade Pavlik: The Rise and Fall of a Soviet Boy Hero* (London, 2005).

8 Taylor and Christie, *Film Factory*, p. 378.

9 David Stirk and Elena Pinto Simon, 'Jay Leyda and *Bezhin Meadow*', in Ian Christie and Richard Taylor, eds, *Eisenstein Rediscovered* (London, 1993), pp. 41–52.

10 Jay Leyda and Zina Voynow, *Eisenstein at Work* (New York, 1982), p. 86.

11 Ibid., p. 86.

12 Taylor and Christie, *Film Factory*, p. 379.

13 Ibid., p. 378.

14 Ibid., p. 379.

15 Ibid., p. 380.

16 Sergei Eisenstein, *Selected Works*, III: *Writings, 1934–47*, ed. Richard Taylor, trans. William Powell (London, 1996), p. 104.

17 Peter Kenez, 'A History of *Bezhin Meadow*', in Al LaValley and Barry P. Scherr, eds, *Eisenstein at 100: A Reconsideration* (New Brunswick, NJ, and London, 2001), p. 206.

18 Barry P. Scherr, 'Alexander Nevsky: Film Without a Hero', in LaValley and Scherr, *Eisenstein at 100*, p. 208.

19 Sergei Eisenstein, *Beyond the Stars: The Memoirs of Sergei Eisenstein*, ed. Richard Taylor, trans. William Powell (London, 1995), p. 740.

20 Scherr, 'Alexander Nevsky', p. 211.

21 Marie Seton, *Sergei M. Eisenstein: A Biography* (London, 1952), p. 386.

22 In sculpture, for example, the border guard made regular appearances in exhibitions, parks and even the metro system. See Mike O'Mahony, *Sport in the USSR: Physical Culture – Visual Culture* (London, 2006), p. 139.

23 Nina Tumarkin, *Lenin Lives! The Lenin Cult in Soviet Russia* (Cambridge, MA, 1983); O'Mahony, *Sport in the USSR*, pp. 38–56.

24 James Goodwin, *Eisenstein, Cinema, and History* (Urbana and Chicago, IL, 1993), p. 174.

25 Goodwin, *Eisenstein*, p. 170.

26 Sergei Eisenstein, *The Film Sense*, ed. Jay Leyda (New York, 1947), p. 158.

27 Sergei Eisenstein, 'My Subject is Patriotism', in Eisenstein, *Selected Works*, III, p. 117. The article was first published anonymously in the English-language journal *International Literature* in 1939.

28 Bulgakowa, *Sergei Eisenstein*, p. 205; Ronald Bergan, *Sergei Eisenstein: A Life in Conflict* (London, 1997), p. 311.

29 Other recent productions included *Peter the First* (*Part I*, 1937; *Part II*, 1939) and *Minin and Pozharsky* (1939).

30 Joan Neuberger, *Ivan the Terrible* (London, 2003), p. 3.

31 'Communist Party Central Committee Decree on the Film A Great Life', in Eisenstein, *Selected Works*, III, pp. 295–8.

32 Published in *Kultura i Zhizn*, 20 October 1946. See Bulgakowa, *Sergei Eisenstein*, p. 228.

33 'Stalin, Molotov and Zhdanov on *Ivan the Terrible*, Part Two', in Eisenstein, *Selected Works*, III, pp. 299–304.

34 'Stalin, Molotov and Zhdanov', p. 303.

35 Goodwin, *Eisenstein, Cinema, and History*, p. 201.

36 Maureen Perrie, *The Cult of Ivan the Terrible in Stalin's Russia* (Basingstoke, 2001).

37 The Battle of Kursk, fought in the summer of 1943 while Eisenstein was shooting *Ivan the Terrible*, is still widely regarded as the biggest tank battle of modern history.

38 Neuberger, *Ivan the Terrible*, p. 2.

39 Goodwin, *Eisenstein, Cinema, and History*, p. 199.

40 Neuberger, *Ivan the Terrible*, p. 106.

41 Ibid.

42 Ibid., p. 92.

43 Ibid., p. 25.

44 Yuri Tsivian, *Ivan the Terrible* (London, 2002), p. 45.

45 Ibid.

46 The interior set design, as Goodwin has pointed out, also bears more than a passing resemblance to the etchings of imaginary prisons produced by the eighteenth-century Italian artist Giovanni Battista Piranesi. See Goodwin, *Eisenstein, Cinema, and History*, p. 211.

47 Sergei Eisenstein, 'From Lectures on Music and Colour in *Ivan the Terrible*', in Eisenstein, *Selected Works*, III, p. 327.

48 Ibid., p. 323.

49 David Bordwell, *The Cinema of Eisenstein*, (London, 2005), p. 190.

50 Bulgakowa, *Sergei Eisenstein*, p. 230.

Epilogue

1 David Bordwell, *The Cinema of Eisenstein* (London, 2005), p. 159.
2 Denise Youngblood, *Movies for the Masses: Popular Cinema and Soviet Society in the 1920s* (Cambridge, 1992), p. 6.
3 Vida T. Johnson, 'Eisenstein and Tarkovsky', and Andrew Barrett, 'In the Name of the Father', in Al LaValley and Barry P. Scherr, eds, *Eisenstein at 100: A Reconsideration* (New Brunswick, NJ and London, 2001), p. 167.
4 Johnson, 'Eisenstein and Tarkovsky', p. 167.
5 Alexander Solzhenitsyn, trans., Ralph Parker, *One Day in the Life of Ivan Denisovich* (Harmondsworth, 1963), pp. 70–71.

Select Bibliography

Aumont, Jacques, *Montage Eisenstein* (Bloomington, IN, 1987)

Barna, Yon, *Eisenstein: The Growth of a Cinematic Genius* (London, 1973)

Beumers, Birgit, ed., *The Cinema of Russia and the Former Soviet Union* (London, 2007)

Bergan, Ronald, *Sergei Eisenstein: A Life in Conflict* (London, 1997)

Bordwell, David, *The Cinema of Eisenstein* (London, 2005)

Bulgakowa, Oksana, *Sergei Eisenstein: A Biography* (Berlin and San Francisco, CA, 1998)

Christie, Ian, and David Elliott, *Eisenstein at Ninety* (Oxford, 1988)

—, and John Gillett, eds, *Futurism, Formalism, FEKS: 'Eccentrism' and Soviet Cinema 1918–36* (London, 1978)

—, and Richard Taylor, eds, *Inside the Film Factory* (London, 1991)

—, eds, *Eisenstein Rediscovered* (London, 1993)

Eisenstein, Sergei, *Film Form: Essays in Film Theory*, ed. and trans. Jay Leyda (New York, 1949)

—, *Selected Works, Volume I: Writings, 1922–34*, ed. and trans. Richard Taylor (London, 1988)

—, *Selected Works, Volume II: Towards a Theory of Montage*, ed. Michael Glenny and Richard Taylor, trans. Michael Glenny (London, 1991)

—, *Beyond the Stars: The Memoirs of Sergei Eisenstein*, ed. Richard Taylor, trans. William Powell (London, 1995)

—, *Selected Works, Volume III: Writings, 1934–47*, ed. Richard Taylor, trans. William Powell (London, 1996)

Geduld, Harry M., and Ronald Gottesman, eds, *Sergei Eisenstein and Upton Sinclair: The Making and Unmaking of Que Viva Mexico!* (Bloomington, IN, and London, 1970)

Goodwin, James, *Eisenstein, Cinema and History* (Urbana and Chicago, 1993)

Hakan, Lövgren, *Eisenstein's Labyrinth: Aspects of a Cinematic Synthesis of the Arts* (Stockholm, 1996)

Karetnikova, Inga, and Leon Steinmetz, *Mexico According to Eisenstein* (New Mexico, 1991)

Kenez, Peter, *Cinema and Soviet Society: From the Revolution to the Death of Stalin* (London, 2001)

Kleberg, Lars, and Hakan Lövgren, *Eisenstein Revisited* (Stockholm, 1987)

LaValley, Al, and Barry P. Scherr, eds, *Eisenstein at 100: A Reconsideration* (New Brunswick, NJ, and London, 2001)

Leyda, Jay, *Kino: A History of the Russian and Soviet Film* (New York, 1960)

—, and Zina Voynow, *Eisenstein at Work* (New York, 1982)

Mally, Lynn, *Culture of the Future: The Prolekult Movement in Revolutionary Russia* (Berkeley, CA, 1990)

Marshall, Herbert, ed., *The Battleship Potemkin* (New York, 1978)

Montagu, Ivor, *With Eisenstein in Hollywood* (New York, 1967)

Nesbet, Anne, *Savage Junctures: Sergei Eisenstein and the Shape of Thinking* (London, 2003)

Neuberger, Joan, *Ivan the Terrible* (London, 2003)

Nizhny, Vladimir, *Lessons with Eisenstein* (New York, 1962)

Richardson, William Harrison, *Mexico Through Russian Eyes, 1806–1940* (Pittsburgh, PA, 1988)

Seton, Marie, *Sergei M. Eisenstein: A Biography* (London, 1952)

Taylor, Richard, *Film Propaganda: Soviet Russia and Nazi Germany* (London, 1979)

—, *Battleship Potemkin* (London, 2000)

—, *October* (London, 2002)

—, and Ian Christie, eds, *The Film Factory: Russian and Soviet Cinema in Documents 1896–1939* (London and New York, 1988)

Taylor, Richard, and Derek Spring, eds, *Stalinism and Soviet Cinema* (London, 1993)

Thompson, Kristen, *Eisenstein's 'Ivan the Terrible': A Neoformalist Analysis* (Princeton, NJ, 1981)

Tsivian, Yuri, *Ivan the Terrible* (London, 2002)

Youngblood, Denise, *Movies for the Masses: Popular Cinema and Soviet Society in the 1920s* (Cambridge, 1992)

—, *The Magic Mirror: Moviemaking in Russia, 1908–1918* (Madison, WI, 1999)

Acknowledgements

This project was generously supported by a University of Bristol Research Fellowship, and I would like to thank my colleagues at Bristol for their support and encouragement. In particular, I want to thank Birgit Beumers, whose support and assistance has been, as ever, exceedingly generous. I also extend my thanks to my postgraduate students who have offered their own views on Eisenstein's work and helped me to shape, and reshape, my own.

Any scholar currently undertaking research into early Soviet cinema, and Eisenstein in particular, owes a huge debt to those whose work has gone before. The pioneering achievements of scholars including Yon Barna, Jay Leyda, Herbert Marshall, Ivor Montagu, Vladimir Nizhny and Marie Seton helped initially to facilitate, and subsequently to shape, Eisenstein studies, while the more recent interventions of Jacques Aumont, Ronald Bergen, David Bordwell, Oksana Bulgakowa, Ian Christie, James Goodwin, Hakan Lövgren, Anne Nesbet, Joan Neuberger, Kristen Thompson and Yuri Tsivian, among many others, have resulted in fascinating new insights into Eisenstein's prodigious output, both literary and cinematic. Special mention should also be made of two individuals whose names have become synonymous with Eisenstein studies. Alongside his incisive and always enlightening analyses of Eisenstein's films and writings, Richard Taylor's monumental work in making the master's writings available to English-speaking audiences has done as much as anyone else's to maintain the Soviet director's significance for future generations. Naum Kleiman has, for half a century now, been one of the foremost scholars and acted as the principal guardian of Eisenstein's legacy for Soviet, post-Soviet and Western audiences.

Finally, I wish to extend an enormous hand of gratitude to my wife, Claire, whose passion for and knowledge of cinema old and new, silent and sound, regional and international, and dramatic and documentary far exceeds my own. It is safe to say that without her wisdom, her insights and, not least, her indulgence in listening to my unformed thoughts on Eisenstein from morning to night, during the working week or over a restful weekend, even while walking the dog, this book would never have happened.

Photo Acknowledgements

The author and publishers wish to express their thanks to the following sources of illustrative material and/or permission to reproduce it:

Photos from the author's collection: pp. 39, 66, 68, 70, 72, 74, 78, 88, 92, 96, 97, 98, 105, 107, 111, 112, 123, 141, 143, 145, 150, 164, 165, 166, 167, 171, 177, 180, 184, 187, 189, 194; photos reproduced courtesy of the Museum of Cinema, Moscow: pp. 6, 13, 22, 34, 37, 41, 57, 59, 89, 119, 121, 126, 130, 137, 197.